This project was funded by:

Published by Sandra Bain
Moorside,
Tore, Muir of Ord,
Ross-shire
IV6 7RY

Typeset and printed by
Lewis Recordings, Drumsmittal,
North Kessock, Inverness

ISBN 0 9514599 5 3

Growing for the Future

The Story of Tore School

Sandra Bain

For Andrew & Eileen

Sandra Bain

Dedicated to the pupils
of
Tore School
past and present
especially to my father
who sadly did not live
to see it published.

CONTENTS

Introduction

Growing for the Future was originally intended to be a celebration of one hundred and twenty-five years of Tore School (1879 to 2004). Research began to raise questions and, although 1879 was when the State took control of the school at Tore, evidence came to light of an earlier establishment.

This book is the story of what most people would consider a fairly ordinary country school; a story which could be duplicated as many times as there are small country primary schools. Yet each school is unique as is each child who goes through its doors. The children are the school, although its influence has an immeasurable bearing upon their lives.

This account brings together many children and teachers and documents many everyday events, ordinary and not-so ordinary, of the past hundred and twenty-five years. Those who are closely involved with the school today will find that there is much which has not changed.

The inclusion of contemporary national and world events is an attempt to set school events against the background of history and to remind children, of all decades, of interesting developments during their childhood and that of their predecessors.

Dramatic fluctuations in the school roll (see page 200) have, at least twice, had the authorities making utterances about closure. The threat in the 1990s saw parents rise to meet the challenge and they worked hard to keep the school open ensuring that the story of Tore School continues.

Abbreviations used

SSPCK	Society in Scotland for the Propagation of Christian Knowledge
HMI	His/Her Majesty's Inspector
MOH	Medical Officer of Health
PE	Physical Education
RE	Religious Education
RNI	Royal Northern Infirmary
POW	Prisoner of War
IQ	Intelligence Quotient
MOT	Ministry of Transport
SRA	Science Research Associates
SMO	Schools Medical Officer

Sketch Map of Tore Area

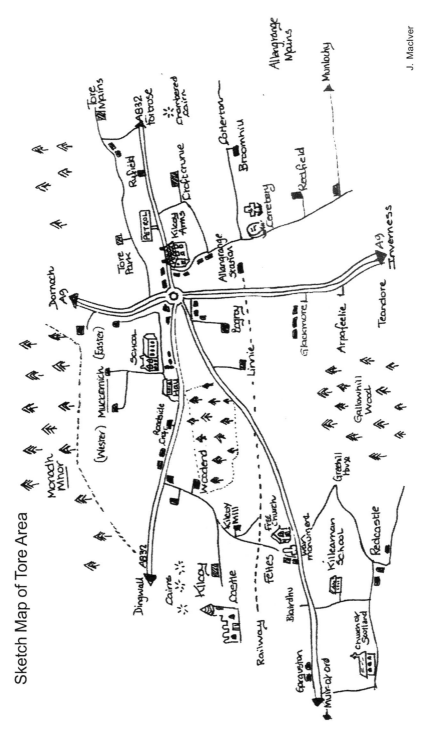

J. MacIver

7

Prologue

Early Education in Scotland

In the 16th Century the Reformation of the Church in Scotland had far-reaching effects on education. The reformers' target was a school in every parish to educate children from five years old up to ten or eleven. The subjects to be taught were Reading, Writing and Arithmetic.

Because of lack of finance it proved difficult to achieve this target and over the following eighty years the Privy Council of the Scottish Parliament passed a number of acts attempting to enforce the setting up of schools in parishes where there were none. Parishioners whether they had children or not were required to support the school financially.

An Act of 1696 remained the basis in Scotland for the parish school system until the 19th Century. The parish schools were Presbyterian in outlook but in the early 19th Century both the Scottish Episcopal Church and the Roman Catholic Church established their own Church Schools. Arpafeelie School, near Glaickmore, originated from the Episcopal Church.

In the mid-18th century a survey of schooling was carried out for the Society in Scotland for the Propagation of Christian Knowledge (SSPCK). Out of one hundred and five parishes fewer than twenty had no parish school. In some areas there were also schools set up by SSPCK and by others.

Early Education in Killearnan

According to the entry, written by Rev David Denoon, in the Statistical Account of 1791-1799 there was in the Parish a school supported by the SSPCK *'where 60-90 children have been taught gratis'*. The schoolmaster's annual salary of £81.6.8d (£81.33) was considered by Denoon to be inadequate. He recorded that the post was vacant,

> *because no qualified person can be got to accept of it. What a pity it is that the pecuniary reward of a description of man, among the most useful in society, should exceed only, in a mere trifle, the wages of a common hireling.*

Minutes of the SSPCK note that the teacher in the school in 1780 was John Noble and there were thirty-five boys and five girls being taught. The school was situated at Croftnacreich which was in those days within the parish boundary of Killearnan but a relatively long distance from Tore. In 1828 John Corbet was the teacher and there were one hundred and twenty-one pupils of whom ninety were boys. Mrs Corbet ran a *'school for spinning, sewing and other female industry'*.

Some time in the early 1800s a petition signed by fifty parents (mainly fathers) was presented to Sir Colin MacKenzie of Kilcoy. Several of the names appear to have been written by the same person, reminding us that many of them would have been unable to read or write. In the 1841 census over forty of the same names appear, most of them with school-age children, so we conclude that the petition dated from around that time.

Unto Sir Colin MacKenzie Bart of Kilcoy the petition of the undersigned inhabitants of the district of Tore and its vicinity humbly sheweth

I That owing to the distance at which we reside from any school our children are quite precluded from the means of Education.
II That in the district to which we belong there are about 100 children who if a school were established amongst us could regularly attend.
III That anxiety for the welfare of our families has urged us to support a teacher at our expense till Whitsuntide.
IV That although we might be able to support a teacher we are quite unable to raise a schoolhouse and in none of our houses is there sufficient accommodation for the number of children who would assemble.
In these circumstances and with feelings of deep respect we beg leave to lay our case before you hoping that the claimant exigencies of our families will not plead in vain in a bosom to whose generosity so many can bear testimony when we humbly beg that you may be pleased to furnish us with the necessary accommodation till Whitsunday, venturing to suggest as a suitable place the kitchen of Tore House with the closet adjoining, which while by its locality and dimension it will amply suit our purpose from its being at present unoccupied can be the most conveniently spared accommodation in the district.

Tore House was situated about two hundred metres west of Tore Mains and appears on an old map as Tore Castle. Along with Kilcoy Castle and Belmaduthy it belonged to the lairds of Kilcoy. At times the widow ladies occupied it. By the 1820s it appears to have been uninhabited.

In *The New Statistical Account* of the mid 19th Century the Killearnan entry, written by Rev John Kennedy, recorded that there were two schools in the Parish. In the parochial school at Redcastle Greek, Latin, English Grammar, Geography and practical Mathematics were taught. The schoolmaster's salary was £30 and he had a house. At the SSPCK School the subjects taught were English, Gaelic, Writing and Arithmetic. The master's pay was £15 with a small croft. The account also mentioned a female school supported by SSPCK. This may have been the one run by Mrs Corbet in 1828. According to the Ordnance Survey of 1872 there was a female school at Milton. There girls were taught and also young children. The schoolmistress received £5 (per year) and school fees were one shilling to four shillings per quarter. Children of the poor were taught free.

In 1843 the Disruption took place when a large number of the ministers, including Donald Kennedy of Killearnan, and their congregations left the Established Church and the Free Church of Scotland was founded.

In August the Kirk Session of the newly formed Redcastle Free Church discussed moves to establish a school at Tore but there is no further reference to this. The parish school continued after the Disruption but teachers who adhered to the Free Church lost their jobs.

By August 1845 steps were being taken to have a school built in the village of Redcastle. In 1847 in the list of deacons of the Free Church were the names of Donald MacKintosh, teacher, Redcastle, and Murdoch Kennedy, teacher, Croftnacreach.

The Free Church school in Killearnan was built near Redcastle Quarry. It was a one-storey building and slated. The remains are still evident. In 1851 the schoolmaster, Alexander MacKenzie, was Clerk to the Deacons' Court of Redcastle Free Church and successive schoolmasters fulfilled the same function.

By 1851 the Free Church Education Committee supported over six hundred schools in Scotland. Around half were new foundations and the rest were schools which had been transferred to the Church.

In the 1871 census there is an entry for Tore School. A teacher, Ann Forbes aged twenty-five, lived there along with Jeanet Forbes aged sixty and Catherine Forbes aged forty, all born in the Parish of Killearnan. In 1844 a daughter, Ann, was born to Donald Forbes and Janet Gollan. In 1851 at the time of the census Ann was staying with her grandparents and Catherine, her aunt, at Kilcoy. It might not be wrong to assume that these entries for Ann Forbes refer to the same person.

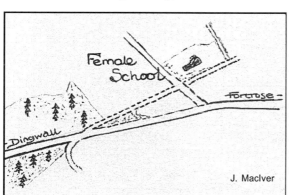

The Ordnance Survey of 1872 indicated a female school on the site of the present school at Tore. Was this the response to the petition? The average daily attendance was about thirty-five and *'the education taught consists of the ordinary branches together with industry'*. The school was solely supported by school fees. The survey was carried out by Robert Greig, parochial schoolmaster in Munlochy, and Mr K.Campbell grocer, Muckernich, but whose address was given as Kessock Ferry.

Education Act 1872

The Argyle Commission of 1864-1867 made a study of education in Scotland and as a result of their findings the Education Scotland Act of 1872 was published:

> *that the means of procuring efficient education for their children may be furnished and made available to the whole people of Scotland.*

The government took over responsibility for schools and compulsory education was established for five to thirteen year olds.

As the Churches and SSPCK handed over education the state undertook to continue daily Religious Instruction. The school day began with an act of Religious Observance (a psalm or hymn and a prayer) followed by Religious Instruction, or Bible Knowledge as it was frequently called.

The Scotch Education Department was a committee of the Privy Council and was based in London. In 1885 responsibility for this Department was transferred to the Secretary of State for Scotland and the new Scottish Office. The name *Scottish* Education Department did not appear until 1918 and it was not until 1939 that it settled in Edinburgh.

The 1872 Act stated that within twelve months a School Board was to be elected in every parish and burgh. Electors were to be of lawful age (twenty-one) and their names must appear on the most recent valuation roll. A School Board would have no less than five members and no more than fifteen.

Scholars had to pay fees but if they were unable to do so they had to apply to the parochial board of the Parish.

It was the duty of the School Board to appoint a defaulting officer to make sure that children attended.

Lands of Tore near the site of Tore 'Big House'

1. Children are what we make them

Our schooldays

Printed on the mount of a school photograph taken in 1953 are the words '*School days are happy days*'. Words which we suspect were written by an adult when time and experience had filtered out the bad memories, and the pressures of adult life had created a hankering for the carefree days of childhood.

We all have mixed memories of life at school. Until relatively recently the first day at school was not softened by time at Playgroup and Nursery but in a child's life it was the first major separation from a mother who was at home all day.

It is surprising to find that even ninety years ago some children were in school before their fourth birthday while others were six or seven years old before they were enrolled.

For many children it was a day eagerly anticipated but for others it was traumatic. How many mothers lost patience with an excited child asking for the umpteenth time when was school starting? Yet school could be a let-down. Instead of sharing toys and significant adults with one or two siblings, in school everything including the teacher's time had to be shared with about thirty others, many of whom were older.

To some children school was an adventure in learning. To others it was a boring disruption to 'real life' and no amount of skill and enthusiasm on the part of the teacher could dispel that attitude.

An afternoon reunion organised at Tore School in 1996 was a time of reminiscences. One of the current pupils reporting on that day wrote, '*We got some good stories from them.*' We remember high points from our time at school and although our Primary schooldays are just about lost in the mists of time memories are stirred when we meet up with old friends and the conversation turns to those days. In talking to a cross-section of former pupils the writer found a wealth of information from past times at Tore School.

Changes

Among today's pupils are descendants of some who attended in the early days. Their school bears little resemblance to the place which their grandparents and great-grandparents knew.

Education has changed considerably since the 19th Century, and the latter part of the 20th Century saw more rapid change than at any time during the previous decades.

Tore Public School, as it was known for nearly a hundred years, has seen many changes. The building itself has been altered and extended several times although we believe that part of the original structure is still there beneath the present façade.

Attitudes have changed. The pupil-teacher relationship has become much more informal. A pupil of the 1920s used to recount how the boys were expected to salute the Headmaster if they met him outside school. The strap (tawse) was considered a deterrent to bad behaviour and idleness until the 1970s when its use was phased out. It is now no longer permitted as punishment or deterrant and the emphasis is on nurturing self-discipline and encouraging positive behaviour.

In today's school are many children from outwith the catchment area, a situation which is possible in this commuter age and under the Parents' Charter of 1988. A hundred years ago when children had to walk to school it would not have been practical to attend an elementary school other than the nearest.

A large number of the early pupils were from the families of farm workers. Most of the others came from homes where there was a croft. Employment among today's parents, while including farming, tends to range across the whole spectrum of professions and trades.

Radio and Television were unheard of in the 19th Century. Children in the 21st Century, through these media, are much more aware of history being made.

Gaelic

In this area most people, children included, spoke both Gaelic and English but the matter of Gaelic in schools was a vexed question in those early days of State education. In the *Ross-shire Journal* on October 31st 1879 Mr Sime, the local HMI (Her Majesty's Inspector) for education, had an article published. He was not favourably disposed to Gaelic and argued the case against its use in schools.

> *There is but one way whereby the Highlander can have the world before him ...that is the knowledge of English.*

This attitude to the language probably contributed to its demise in the next generation – the sons and daughters of those early children in Tore School. Parents, although Gaelic speakers, tended to use the language to communicate with each other but not with their children. It was a convenient way of keeping from the children things they shouldn't hear. If English was considered a guarantee of future success it is easy to see why parents would encourage its use at the expense of what probably was their own first language.

Many Gaelic words survived alongside English in this locality: examples are *bùrach* (an untidy mess) and an (old) man was never anything else but a *bodach* and a woman was always a *cailleach*. It was a long time before this writer realised that these were not English words.

2. The First Decade

On 27th October 1879 Tore Public School opened. Responsibility for running it was in the hands of Killearnan Public School Board, a group of men of standing in the Parish – ministers, farmers, business men – who already had experience of running the Public School at Redcastle (also known as Killearnan School).

1879 was the year of the War in South Africa when British troops fought the Zulus over the matter of the border with Natal. It was also the year of the Afghan War. The *Ross-shire Journal* of 31st October reported on both of these wars including the news that Kabul, the capital of Afghanistan, had been taken earlier in the month.

Eleven children enrolled that first week in the new school. They were probably unaware of many of the events going on in the wider world. An American called Thomas Edison was demonstrating his invention of an electric light bulb. To those children electricity would not even be a dream. More than seventy years were to pass before the children of Tore would do their lessons by any artificial light other than that of a paraffin lamp.

The only shops they knew were the local general merchants so a special five cents store opened by F.W. Woolworth in USA in 1879 would be of no interest had they even heard about it. It was not, however, going to be many years before a trip to Inverness for a special treat would include a visit to 'Woollies' where everything cost 6d (2½p). Woolworth's had come to the Highlands.

In addition to reporting news of world and national events that issue of the *Ross-shire Journal* contained a few snippets of school news but there was no mention that a school had opened in Tore.

Two of the many advertisements in the paper, which incidentally cost one Penny (about ½p in today's money), were the following.

> *Boys' Readymade Trousers from 2s 6d to 5s 9d*
> *Skirts Kilted, Braided and Trimmed, with Alpacca, Cord,*
> *Felt, and Satin from 4s 6d to 13s 6d*

One shilling (1s) was the equivalent of 5p in today's money. We understand that prices rose very little until after World War II.

Running the School

The Scotch Education Department operated from Whitehall and it was to them that Killearnan Public School Board was responsible for the running of the schools in the Parish – Redcastle (sometimes known as Killearnan) which was already open and Tore. The Clerk of the School Board was Mr George MacLennan, Achnasoul, in the Parish of Urray. Rev Neil Gillies, minister of the Free Church, who had been ordained and inducted on 7th August 1872, was one of the members and he was a very diligent visitor to the school. He was about thirty years old at the time. There is little mention of Rev William MacKay who was Parish Church minister then.

The schoolmaster appointed to the new school was John Tuach. Until 6th June 1879 a lad of this name had been one of two Pupil Teachers in Killearnan School. He was discharged *'by order of the School Board they having considered that two Pupil Teachers were unnecessary'*. He had completed four years. It seems too much of a coincidence that there would be two teachers by the name of John Tuach in the same neighbourhood.

Pupil teachers were young people from age thirteen, interested in teaching, who worked with class teachers and at the same time studied for examinations. A letter of 27th December 1901 from the Scotch Education Department contained instructions regarding their exam. This was to take place in May of their second and fourth years. Candidates were provided with an exercise book and blotting paper but were expected to provide their own pens. The letter also mentioned the King's Scholarship Examination. Successful candidates in that exam were awarded £20 or £25. On the occasion of His Majesty's Inspector's visit Pupil Teachers were tested in Reading, Recitation and Teaching and Music and (in the case of the girls) Needlework.

At the end of four or five years, on passing their examinations, they usually attended Teacher Training College (Normal School) to qualify as certificated teachers. Those Colleges were in the hands of the Church until 1905 when they were taken over by the Scotch Education Department.

The Building

In the 1882 record of disposal of land at Tore to Killearnan School Board, mention was made of the building on the site.

The Ordnance Survey of 1872 described that building, at that time a female school, as *'one story high, thatched and in fair repair'*.

The School Board was instructed to remove the thatched roof and build a slated roof. In a later report when reconstruction was being carried out we read of a clay floor, found under the current floor. The building may have been of rough stone, like the early croft houses. The annual feu duty levied in 1882 was to be four pounds four shillings (four guineas).

There was one classroom and living accommodation for the teacher, at the west end. According to the 1901 census there were three rooms with windows which was corroborated in a comment by a former pupil of the early 1900s who wrote that in addition to the schoolroom there were two rooms, one upstairs and another downstairs, for the teacher.

An entry in the Log Book recorded that the dimensions of the schoolroom 'were *30' 6''* (about 9 metres) *long, 16' 6''* (5m) *wide with 11'* (3.5m) *high walls and 14'* (4.2m) *high ceiling'*.

It was heated by a single fireplace at the east end. This was lit and kept stoked by the teacher. Although not specifically mentioned it is likely that, as happened in other areas, the children took a peat to school for the fire. The peat bog for the community was in the area known as Millbuie Common (or 'The Moss') on the right hand side of the road to Dingwall. The track to the peat is opposite the Drynie Park road. Until the 1950s local people dug peat there.

The seats were forms without backs and there was mention of these in Inspectors' reports well into the 20th Century. They are visible in the group photo of 1920-21. Two weeks after the school opened Mr Tuach noted in the school Log Book that little progress had been made as the school was not yet supplied with a blackboard.

He did not seem pleased with the standard of work his pupils were producing, recording that Standards I and II were backward in Arithmetic and that Standards III and IV were backward in Grammar. By December Standards I, II and III had improved in both subjects. There was no mention of Standard IV.

Classes

Schools had two levels of Infants – Lower Infants and Higher Infants (now known as Primary 1 and Primary 2). This was followed by Standards I to IV, equivalent to the current Primary 3 to 6. At a later stage, possibly 1881, Standard V was added and around 1903 a Supplementary Class, or Standard VI, became common (although not until later in Tore). These senior classes disappeared when all pupils were required to attend Secondary School and later the terms 'Infant' and 'Standard' were to be replaced by the designation 'Class' or 'Primary'.

An examination by the School Board in 5th May 1880 indicated that Standards II, III and IV 'did good' while the performance of Standard I and under was fair.

On September 1st, 1880, fourteen pupils went along to the Public School at Killearnan where Mr Jolly, Her Majesty's Inspector (HMI), tested the children. Mr Tuach recorded in the weeks preceding this examination that he was giving special drill in certain areas of the work.

On 26th October he wrote in the Log Book:

> *Report from Education Department in connection with the annual inspection conducted by Mr Jolly in the public School Killearnan on September 1st.*
> *'The Tore pupils did well for a first appearance.*
> *No of children presented – 14*
> *13 passed in reading, 10 in writing and 11 in Arithmetic.*
> *No of passes 34 at 6/-' £10.4 amount of grant received.*

The grant depended not just on the number of pupils on the school roll but also on their performance in the annual inspection so it is understandable that the teacher would spend much time preparing his pupils.

Attendance

From the original eleven pupils, the school roll gradually increased but the picture emerging from the Log Book was one of rather erratic attendance. There were a number of factors contributing to this. With any sign of bad weather, whether it be windy and wet or a full-blown snowstorm, many of the children were unable to attend school.

This was (and still is) a rural area where children live at some distance from the school and those were the days before minibuses to transport the scholars. Children all walked to school. Their clothes would probably not be waterproof and during the spring and summer months they went to school barefooted.

Three Victorian schoolboys
From a photograph by N.U.T.

With only one fire to warm the classroom there might be little heat reaching the children, especially if they sat at the far end, and they could be sitting in wet clothes all day.

Mr Tuach recorded poor attendance for the week ending 20th February 1880. On Monday and Tuesday the weather was unsettled and later in the week the Muir-of-Ord market took place. It was not in pursuit of some fun that children went along. They would be required to herd cattle being taken for sale. The *Ross-shire Journal* of October 31st 1879 reported the markets as being Wednesday and Thursday – sheep on Wednesday and cattle and horses on Thursday. The market, held monthly, took place on the south side of Muir-of-Ord where the Golf Course is now situated. In the Edinburgh Almanac of 1888 it was described as the most important cattle fair in the north of Scotland. There was also an annual cattle fair in May (on the Monday after the first Wednesday) at *Croftcrunny of Kilcoy*. The 1872 Ordnance Survey showed Tore Market Stance in front of the Kilcoy Arms Inn (the old Inn).

Harvest

It may seem strange that the opening of the school took place so late in the year but in Victorian times the long summer holidays started in August or early September and went on until late October. This was designed to cover the time of harvest and potato lifting. In later records they are sometimes called the 'harvest holidays'. Children were needed for agricultural tasks and at a time when wages, especially those of farm workers, were low any money which the children could earn would be very welcome in the home.

Stooks at Tore Village early last century

We should remember that corn-cutting (and at this time oats was the main crop grown in this area) was done by hand with sickle or scythe. It was gathered into bundles (sheaves) and bound by a 'rope' made by twisting stalks of corn together. Six or eight sheaves were then propped against each other into stooks to dry. When they were considered to be dry they were loaded on to a horse-drawn cart and brought to the stackyard where they were carefully placed in round stacks to await the threshing mill.

Over the years the Log Book contains many references in different seasons to the attendance problems created by children being kept out of school to help with farm-work, including going to the market. The times of harvest and potato lifting, which tended to occur after school resumed in October, were the worst but for two weeks in May that first year the teacher recorded low attendance 'on account of the potato planting and the turnips'. This reference to turnips was likely to concern the sowing of the seed.

Around the end of November or beginning of December a day (always a Thursday) was given as a holiday for Harvest Thanksgiving. In the first year of the school Thursday 27th November was the appointed day. All Churches in the Parish observed the same day so that children and teachers were able to attend, indeed were expected to attend, a service in their Church.

The date of this holiday varied from year to year presumably because they had to wait until the harvest was complete. A report in the *Ross-shire Journal* indicated that the Presbytery determined which Thursday was to be set aside for the Harvest Thanksgiving.

The tradition of Thursday holiday continued until the 1950s by which time Harvest Thanksgiving services were being changed to Sunday or to a

Thursday evening. Until very recently, in some congregations in the Highlands, Thursday evening continued to be the time designated.

Farming

A former pupil who was born in 1895 thought that all the children in his day came from the families of farm workers or crofters. His father was grieve in Croftcrunie and, earning nineteen shillings per week, he had responsibility for much of the farm's business.

Certainly many of the children in the school were from families of farm workers. Although some men remained with the same farmer for many years others changed their employment frequently. This took place at *the Term* which was May and November. The *feeing* market was the place to negotiate terms with a new employer. A man might decide to move for more pay, for promotion to cattleman or grieve, or because his wife didn't like the place. He might be offered a better house on another farm. The reputation of the local school would have had little importance.

When families moved, all their belongings were piled on to a horse-drawn cart and the children were found a space. A woman who grew up in a neighbouring parish and whose father was a farm worker recalls seeing all their furniture and other possessions being loaded on to a cart. On one occasion her mother and the children were transported in the farmer's car – an 'Overland'. Her father was moving to a position as grieve.

Jean Cameron who was a pupil in Tore School in the 1930s remembers once getting up early on the day of *the Term* and, with her brothers and sisters, watching the flittings. They counted fourteen that day, going in different directions.

When a family was moving the children tended to be absent from school for several days before and after the move. As a result their education was disrupted and they fell behind in their lessons. This situation was exacerbated when they were kept at home to help with farm work.

With progress in farm machinery the number of farm workers decreased. At the present time the only children in the school with farming connections are the farmers' own children.

Christmas and New Year

The last week of 1879 was very stormy. The children were not on holiday, even on 25th December, but attendance was poor because of the weather. On the night of 28th December, a very wild night, the railway bridge across the Firth of Tay from Fife to the city of Dundee collapsed as a train was crossing. All seventy-five passengers and crew on board lost their lives.

Thursday 1st January 1880 was a holiday for New Year's Day and the following week 5th to 12th January was designated the 'Christmas holiday'.

Entries in the Log Book for several years recorded New Year holidays around 12th January. The history of this lies in a date change put into effect in Britain in 1752 to bring the calendar into line with the seasons. The day following 2nd September was named 14th September which meant that what should have been 25th December became 5th January and what should have been 1st January became 12th January. The Presbyterian Highlands of the 18th and 19th Centuries did not make a great celebration of Christmas but many families continued to celebrate old New Year's Day.

A child of the twenties, from a neighbouring parish, remembers crofters celebrating old New Year's Day on the 12th January. On the farms, only essential work would be carried out, such as feeding animals. Some of the older generation today still refer to 12th January as 'old New Year's Day'.

Within living memory children in the Black Isle hung up their stockings on Hogmanay. In the 1920s presents were small – an orange or an apple, two or three sweets, a penny (which would buy a small bar of chocolate).

Until the 1950s Christmas Day was a working day. The Garage and the Smiddy were open, as was the Pub. Men went to their work during the day but in most families, especially where there were children, there was a celebration in the evening – possibly with members of the extended family.

The Soirée

There were no Christmas parties for the children at school but in 1880 Thursday 25th March was a holiday to allow for preparation for the Sunday School soirée which was held in Killearnan School. Adults spent much time preparing the room, setting up tables with the kind of food which few of the children saw in their homes. Killearnan School was closed the following day to enable 'the schoolroom to be washed out'. Although Mr Tuach did not specify, later records indicated that at these events there was singing and recitation – probably by the children. Another entertainment for the children was the Magic Lantern show. This was an early type of film show where painted slides were projected on to a wall. In an age when there were few treats an evening like that of the soirée would have been very exciting for the children.

At later dates Tore School hosted their own soirée although in some instances there was no indication as to who was running it, whether it was school or Sunday School.

1880-81

The school reopened after the 'summer' holidays on the week of 29th October and 'the most of the time this week has been occupied in arranging of classes'.

An Inspector paid an unannounced visit to the school just after the holidays. His report received on 24th November read,

> *The School was opened for the first time after the vacation on Monday last and Registers have not been kept this week. The offices are very filthy.*

The *'offices'* were the dry lavatories which, we understand, the teacher had to look after. The toilets were, until the 1960s, located outside at the back of the school.

Curriculum

In the early days of education the curriculum was basically Reading, Writing and Arithmetic. Below are two addition sums of the time. This money system of pounds (£), shillings(s) and pence (d) was in use until 1971. The Imperial system of measurement, in yards (yds), feet (ft) and inches (ins) survived much longer.

£	s	d		yd	ft	in
2	3	8		2	2	9
1	16	10		3	2	5
4	0	6		6	2	2

There were 12 pence in 1 shilling and 20 shillings in 1 pound. Measurements of length were 12 inches in 1 foot and 3 feet in 1 yard.

Until well into the 1940s Infants did their early written work on slates – with squeaky pencils. It is likely that in the 1880s all the children used slates since there was no reference to exercise books or lead pencils until the 1890s.

There seems to have been a shortage of reading-books in certain classes and Inspectors were quick to note this and express their criticism.

In a classroom in the very early days it was customary to have a map of the world. Geography and History both had their place in the curriculum.

Victorian classrooms also had a Modulator hanging on the wall. This had the Solfa scale – *doh, ra, me, fah, soh, lah, te, doh* – which was used when learning tunes. In one early Inspector's report there was a comment that the pupils' singing should be sweeter and later a teacher noted the commencement of work from the Solfa notation. A pupil of the 1960s recalls how much she hated the work with the Modulator.

The fear of the Lord is the beginning of wisdom.

There were frequent visits to the school from the Free Church minister, Rev Neil Gillies, who was a member of the School Board. He usually checked the register of attendance and also took Scripture lessons. One of the conditions on which the Church handed education over to the state in 1872 was that the teaching of Religious Knowledge would be a compulsory part of the curriculum. Parents could withdraw their children from these lessons if they wished but there seem to have been very few instances of this happening.

The Religious Knowledge syllabus contained a considerable amount and variety of work. Catechism, Metrical Psalms and portions of Scripture had to be memorised and stories from the Bible were studied. This work continued at least until the sixties in Ross-shire schools. In the past there was great emphasis on memory work in all areas of the curriculum. The school year ended with a Bible Exam and prizegiving. For many years a Bible was given as a prize not only for Bible Knowledge but also for attendance.

The responsibility for examining Religious Knowledge was in the hands of the local ministers and not a task of the school Inspector. The root of this lay in the Churches having had responsibility for early education.

Well into the 20th Century the day began with the singing of a hymn (or psalm) and the Lord's Prayer. All these were learned orally by listening to the older children. One little girl, for a long time, thought the words of a hymn were, 'Hosanna loud as Alice....' until she realised it should be 'Hosanna! Loud Hosannas.....'

Communion (or Sacrament) Holidays

On the last Sunday in February the local Churches celebrated Communion and the children had five days' holiday at that time. Whether the holiday was for the benefit of the children, most of whom probably did attend Church, or for the benefit of the master we don't know.

There was a series of preparatory services starting on Thursday, the *fast-day* although there is no evidence that it was a day of going without food. On each of the days of the Communion weekend there were Gaelic and English services. The actual Communion service was on Sunday and on Monday there was a thanksgiving service.

The second weekend of July was also a Communion weekend when the children again had days off – the long summer holidays did not begin until the end of August.

Church services were generally held at noon and 6 o'clock or 6.30 in the evening, fitting in with feeding times for animals. This was true all year round and no farmer or farm worker would have dreamt of doing anything other than essential work on Sunday.

Census

On 4th April 1881 the children had a holiday because their teacher was an enumerator for the national census which took place that weekend. The area which John Tuach covered, in the Parish of Killearnan, spread east from the school as far as Colinton (between Tore Mains and Muirton Farm), Teanahuig and back west to Tore Inn. At this time the area of Tore Village to the south of the Dingwall Road was part of the Parish of Knockbain as was the area of Muckernich to the west of the school.

John Tuach himself does not appear in the Killearnan census which may indicate that he forgot to count himself or he gave himself a different designation. The only person by that name appearing in any census returns for the whole of the United Kingdom was an *unemployed farm labourer* living at Tore Park. His age was given as twenty-one which would have been about the same as that of the teacher.

The 1901 census records a man John Tuach, born in Killearnan and aged forty-four, living in Inverness. His occupation was given as retired teaplanter.

1881 - 82

Change of Teacher

During the ten years of the 1880s there was considerable turnover of staff – five different teachers. The 1881 summer holidays started on the 23rd August and the first change came when the school reopened on 24th October. Miss Helen Stewart replaced Mr Tuach. At the time of the census a few months earlier a twenty-four-year-old teacher, Helen Stewart, was living at Achduart in the Parish of Lochbroom. She belonged to Edinburgh. Could she be the lady who came to Tore?

That year, because of a late potato harvest, attendance which was as low as eleven or twelve scarcely rose for about a month. On November 29th Mr Cameron, a member of the School Board, recorded that there were twenty children present when he visited the school. The roll at the time was at least forty-two.

The school closed on 31st December for *'Xmas holidays'* and opened on January 10th 1882.

An important world event of 1882 was the isolation of the tuberculosis bacillus (cause of TB) by Robert Koch. TB was a major killer in Scotland well into the 20th Century but his discoveries ensured that more recent generations would be almost free from the disease. In spite of its virulence there is only one reference in the Log Book to children being absent suffering from the illness. Were country children less susceptible? Koch discovered the cholera bacilli in 1883 and the *Ross-shire Journal* of 26th December, 1890, carried an article about him and his contribution to health, and included a photograph, a rarity in the newspapers of that time.

On April 15th mention was made of the fact that some of the older children were leaving school *'for the season'*. On July 5th the entry referred to the examination by Her Majesty's Inspector *'in Redcastle Castle'*. Was this wishful thinking on Miss Stewart's part or a slip of her pen? The examination was held in Redcastle School (Killearnan).

1882-83

In 1883 Miss Williamina Watson replaced Miss Stewart. Her appointment was noted by Neil Gillies on 2nd April. She was just twenty-one years old at this time having been born in May 1861 in Whitehills in Banffshire. She was an adherent of the Free Church and had attended Whitehills Public School where she became a pupil teacher. In 1881-82 she was a student at the Church of Scotland Training College in Aberdeen. Her photograph is one of a group in the reception area of Aberdeen University Education Department but unfortunately there is no individual identification.

In her first week in the school Miss Watson recorded, *'Arithmetic and Grammar are very backward in Standards III, IV, and V.'*

The year 1883 saw the publication of Robert Louis Stevenson's book *Treasure Island*. It is remembered with affection by generations of children who read it for themselves or had it read to them in school.

1883-84

In November an official – probably one of the School Board members – reported:

> *Visited this school and have much pleasure in observing a marked improvement in every branch of teaching under the management of Miss Watson. The attendance is below average only 16 children being present. After potato gathering the attendance is expected to improve.*

An HMI report received in January 1884 was somewhat different in tone.

> *Up to the third Standard inclusive fair work is done in this school. The pupils in fourth and fifth standards know very little. On the day of my visit; a wet one and bitterly cold, there was no fire in the room. The Schedules were not ready, Log Book contained no entry of later date than 10th October 1882 (did he mean 1883?), and the dates in the Register of Attendances were imperfect. No Industrial work has been taught since the holidays. Ventilators & a large grate should be provided. The Walls should be whitewashed and the pupils prevented from writing on them.*

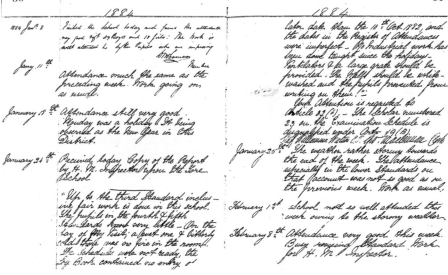

Pages from the Log Book January/February 1884 containing
Inspector's Report dated January 24th

The school leaving age was raised to fourteen in 1883. Only larger towns offered post-Primary education so children generally remained at their Elementary school. Many senior pupils from Tore, even up to the 1920s, went to Killearnan for their final year. The curriculum there catered for children up to the age of fourteen.

In 1884 the National Society for the Prevention of Cruelty to Children was founded in Britain. At a later date the Scottish arm was founded and it is now known as Children 1st. Pupils of the 20th and 21st Centuries have participated in fundraising events for this society.

At Wimbledon that year Maude Watson (no relation to the teacher) won the first women's singles championship.

Because New Year's Day (that was old New Year's Day) fell on a Saturday the 1884 holiday was Monday 14th January. There was no mention of a Christmas holiday.

An Inspector was again at the school between 11th and 21st February. There were fifty-two pupils present, all being taught by one young teacher. After the HMI Examination classes were arranged. There were no details of the arrangement but we suspect that pupils were moved into classes according to progress. The HMI report on 14th March indicated:

The present teacher found the school in very poor condition and has improved it very considerably. Much, however, remains to be done before the higher standards can be said to be efficient. Singing should be sweeter. It should be noted that of 57 on

the roll there are 29 in an average attendance and 28 presented
for the examination. All names and ages should appear in the
Admissions Register. Something should be done to improve
the condition of the playground. Ventilation must in some
manner be supplied.

This presented Miss Watson with some challenges.

On 25th July pupils and teacher were taken on a trip to a neighbouring parish. There were no details given as to where. It may seem little now for children to go to a neighbouring parish but in 1884 it would have been an adventure. We can imagine the excitement of the children – especially the younger ones – having a day off school and being taken, probably by horse and cart, to a place with which they were not familiar.

1884 - 85

Only sixteen pupils turned up on the first day after the summer holiday. Because of repairs to the school that holiday was about a week longer than in previous years. Perhaps the School Board had followed the Inspector's advice and arranged for the walls to be whitewashed or it may have been that the thatch was being replaced by slates as demanded in the title deeds.

After his visit for the session, in February 1885, the Inspector reported, *'The building has been materially improved since last inspection.'*

However that same report indicated that, *'unless each class has at least two sets of Reading books by the next inspection the grant may be reduced.'* *Royal Readers* was a series used in some schools at the time.

The year 1885 produced some noteworthy inventions. Karl Benz invented the first practical car powered by combustion engine, research on radio broadcasts was started by Heinrich Rudolph Hertz and Francis Galton discovered the idea of fingerprinting.

Having taught for just over two years in Tore School, Miss Watson resigned on 5th June 1885. Monday 8th June was a holiday for the children because of the change of teacher and on the following day Jane Middleton took up the post. The marriage of Williamina Watson and William McIntosh, a carpenter from Redcastle, took place on 25th June at Whitehills. They made their home at Rivulet Cottage in Milton and by 1891 they had three daughters. At that time women were not permitted to teach after marriage. A later entry for Williamina McIntosh (Miss Watson) in the College records gave her address as Dunbeath in Caithness.

Coincidentally William McIntosh, a younger man, who was Headmaster at Killearnan school, also lived at Rivulet Cottage.

A public examination of children attending Tore School took place in Killearnan School on 21st August. From later entries we know that this annual event was a Scripture examination before members of the School Board and was frequently attended by parents.

In 1885 the school was closed for summer holidays from 21st August to 5th October. When classes resumed in October only eighteen children were present and all through November attendance was low because of the potato lifting.

In this year the Scottish Office was created as part of the United Kingdom government at Whitehall and, with it, the position of Secretary of State for Scotland. The area responsible for education continued to be known as the Scotch Education Department.

January of 1886 brought very stormy weather and attendance at one point was only eleven out of a roll of over fifty. By February Jessie Forbes, holder of a Provisional Certificate, was the teacher and she signed the Inspector's report.

According to an entry in the 1881 census Jessie Forbes, a farmer's daughter aged twenty-three, was a visitor at the Old Schoolhouse, Rathven, where her sister Eliza was boarding. Eliza and most of the other residents in the house were teachers or pupil teachers. This evidence points to the possibility of Jessie being the woman who five years later came to Tore. She and Eliza were born in Macduff, Banffshire.

Her Majesty's Inspector reported on 6th April, following a visit on 12th February.

> *So many changes of teacher have taken place during the year that the school has been examined at considerable disadvantage. In the circumstances it has done very fairly in most respects and by another year Miss Forbes will no doubt have worked it up to a satisfactory state of efficiency.*

In 1886 Coca-cola was first produced in America. We wonder how long it took before this drink reached Britain and how much longer to reach the Black Isle.

Of more importance that year to the people of Killearnan was the Crofters' Holding Act giving them security of tenure and empowering a Crofters' Commission to fix fair rents.

On July 5th William McIntosh, a member of the School Board, visited the school and recorded in the Log Book, *'Children smart, orderly and attentive.'* He was possibly the man who was married to Miss Watson.

1886 - 1887

In November there was the first mention of children being absent for turnip lifting and at the beginning of December a severe snowstorm meant greatly reduced attendance. That storm seems to have lasted for some time – the entry a week later noted that the weather was still stormy and attendance was still low.

The school was closed for New Year holidays from Thursday 30th December to Tuesday 4th January 1887 and on Wednesday 12th (old New Year's Day) the children were *'taken to attend a treat given for their benefit in the neighbouring parish'.*

At the beginning of March another severe snowstorm meant that only four pupils were present on Friday 11th and the school closed.

A week later the children's soirée was held in the school.

It seems that the Inspector's prediction that Miss Forbes would raise standards was not fulfilled. In his report of April 1st he wrote,

> *Excellent order is present in this school but the state of instruction cannot be regarded as satisfactory. More energy should be thrown into the work and every effort made to see greater regularity of attendance.*
>
> *No children who have not passed the fifth standard should be struck off the register unless they have left the district or are known to be attending another school.*

A week later the teacher made the first recorded mention of a visit from the defaulting officer, Alexander MacLennan, who called at the school to enquire about absentees. The appointment of a defaulting officer (commonly called the 'whipper-in') was mandatory under the 1872 Act. Did it really take the Killearnan School Board nine years to make an appointment? From that time the record of visits was frequent – every ten to fourteen days. For the parents of absentees the penalty seems to have been £1 (more than a month's wage) or up to fourteen days imprisonment. The scheme was fairly ineffective since pupils continued to be absent, helping with various aspects of farm work. The extra labour was welcomed by the farmer at busy times and parents who had crofts also needed extra help. Defaulting officers were poorly paid and they could not afford to alienate parents.

Queen Victoria celebrated her Golden Jubilee on 20th June 1887 but no mention was made in the school Log Book so we assume the children were not granted the holiday which has become customary for such occasions.

On July 22nd Mr MacLennan, Clerk to the School Board, called with five new maps for school use. These were about the only 'pictures' or visual aids to be found in the early schools.

The schoolmistress was absent on August 5th and the work was carried on by a substitute. Until then the absence of the teacher had meant a holiday for the children.

1887 - 88

When the school reopened, on 3rd October, after the summer holidays there were only twelve children present *'owing to the prevalence of whooping-cough in the district'.* Stormy weather followed and then it was time for the potato lifting. This meant that attendance did not pick up until the third week in November.

It was an age when medical treatment had to be paid for and medication was in its infancy. No doubt most homes applied natural remedies for coughs and colds.

An advertisement in the *Ross-shire Journal* in the 1880s was headed *'Throat irritation and Cough'*. There followed a description of Eppa's Glycerine Jujubes which were said to work wonders for the affliction.

Infection spread rapidly in homes where there were large families, housed in few rooms. There were frequent references to epidemics of infectious diseases such as measles and whooping cough.

In December the teacher noted, *'the alteration of the seats a very great improvement to the working of the several classes.'* Considering the layout of a Victorian classroom with its rows of forms it is difficult to imagine what rearranging could have been done. We suspect the seats remained as they were while the children were moved.

On 18th January 1888 the school received a visit from Angus Cameron, of St John's Arpafeelie. That was the only recorded visit of the minister of the Episcopal Church. The school at Arpafeelie was founded by the Episcopal Church but was likely to have been in State control by that time.

In the report from HMI Mr Syme after a visit in February the grant was noted as £36. 5. 0, considerably more than it had been nine years previously. The average attendance was about forty-three.

The school closed on the afternoon of Wednesday 4th April and remained closed on Thursday 5th April because of the children *'having a social meeting in the school room'*. This suggests that the annual soirée was being held on Wednesday evening and on Thursday the schoolroom was being cleaned up.

During the week of May 18th attendance was very low (about thirty-two) because of sickness. At the beginning of June chickenpox was recorded.

Eastman produced the first Kodak camera in 1888, making photography accessible to amateurs. The film was sealed inside so the whole camera had to be sent back for developing. In 1900 he introduced the first Brownie camera – a box camera from which the film could be removed for processing.

1888 - 89

As usual in October, when school resumed after the summer holidays, many children were absent because of the harvest. That situation did not improve for several weeks and towards the end of November children were still absent, lifting potatoes. The defaulting officer called regularly at the school, as did Mr Trotter, Chairman of the School Board. Attempts were being made to enforce attendance but they were unlikely to be effective as long as the farmers needed the children's labour.

December 24th and 25th were given that year, for the first time, as Christmas holidays and, as was customary, 31st December and 1st January were the New Year holidays.

County Councils were established in 1889 but it would be another twenty-nine years before education would become their responsibility.

After the Inspector's visit in February the grant was reduced by ten per cent. His report was as follows:

> *The condition of this small school was complained of last year and it is to be regretted that no improvement is shown this year.*
>
> *Payment of Grant for 'English' and for the lower classes is recommended with much hesitation. The only good feature is Reading – the other subjects of Examination (especially Arithmetic) being decidedly weak.*
>
> *My Lords has ordered a deduction of one-tenth to be made from the Grant on account of faults of instruction.*

Robert Trotter was Chairman of the School Board and was present at the inspection. He was farmer at Garguston as his father had been before him. Mr Trotter who was a Gaelic and English speaker was in his mid forties at the time.

An interesting leaflet which arrived in the school was, *Elementary Science – Navigation.* Even children below Standard II were expected to be able to use the Mariner's Compass and carry out work using a globe *'and on boats'.* Much of Ross and Cromarty is on the sea coast and bearing in mind that Lewis was then part of the County it is not surprising that this subject was part of the curriculum.

Mr William Fraser became defaulting officer in May 1889 replacing Alexander MacLennan, the first recorded attendance officer in the Killearnan School Board area.

In that same year John Dunlop's company began the manufacture of air-filled bicycle tyres and by 1906 was making car tyres. Until Dunlop's invention, tyres were of solid rubber. At that stage there was no mention of children cycling to school but by the middle of the 20th Century most children had a bicycle and cycling proficiency tests were introduced.

1889 - 90

According to the *Ross-shire Journal* of 25th October 1889 John Robertson, who was HMI for Caithness, Sutherland and Easter Ross, was appointed to the mainland Inverness area in place of Mr Syme who had died. Alan Lobban was to take over the northern area in December.

On December 3rd 1889 notice was given that the annual inspection would take place in June instead of February and that the school year would end on 31st May 1890. The holidays would not begin until August.

February 1890 was noted for illness. On the 10th the school had to be closed , *'by orders of N. Gillies owing to the prevalence of influenza among the children'.* The *Ross-shire Journal* of 21st February referred to this epidemic which continued for about a month. Half the world's population was affected by that outbreak.

The *Inverness Courier* in March contained an item about the opening of the Forth Railway Bridge. One of the first cantilever bridges, it was opened on 3rd March 1890 and for several years it was the world's longest span. The opening of the bridge meant a direct journey could be made from Inverness to Edinburgh. Until then travellers by train had to disembark at Burntisland and cross on the ferry, joining a train at the other side which would transport them in to Edinburgh.

Victorian 'Teenager'

HMI Alan Lobban examined the pupils on Monday 9th June and the following four days were given as holiday *'as ordered by Chairman of School Board'*. Mr Lobban's report was received on October 24th. In it, among the usual remarks, he described the children as talkative.

In July the school was closed from 22nd (Tuesday) all week because of the *'severe illness of the teacher'*.

We note that school fees were abolished in 1890. That year also saw the end of payment by results which must have been a relief to teachers, especially those in a community where attendance was not very good.

3. The Nineties

1890 - 91

Miss Helen Macdonald took over as teacher in October 1890 although there is no reference in the Log Book to Miss Forbes leaving. Miss Macdonald was born in Dufftown in 1866 so when she came to Tore she was about twenty-four years old.

The school was a week late in opening after the holidays because of illness among the children and when it did open only four boys and one girl were present. Although in the first entry the nature of the illness was unspecified, just over a week later the Board ordered the school to be closed again for two weeks because of an epidemic of measles. Illness and the harvest caused the attendance to remain low for nearly a month. Measles continued until the end of the year and, in addition, early in December the girls' attendance was down because of colds.

The Inspector's report for 1890 had arrived on 24th October. In it he indicated that Reading was the best feature of the school.

> *Writing and Figuring showed traces of care but poor in style and quality... Arithmetic is unusually weak...Needlework is pretty fair, but more practice should be given in the several testing exercises and the Board should supply material for this purpose. Singing is sweet and tuneful but the children not sufficiently advanced to earn the higher grant... Registers must be kept more carefully and the returns more accurately given in future.*

The first few months of 1891 seem to have been characterised by continuing poor attendance resulting from a combination of bad weather and illness.

The entry dated January 23rd recorded, *'Owing to a severe storm the attendance for this week has been very poor.'* The *Ross-shire Journal* of that week reported this bad weather which was general over the whole country. Locally, there had been a snowstorm on Monday night and Tuesday and, according to the paper, it had snowed in the Black Isle until 7 pm on Wednesday. It continued at intervals all night and there were concerns about sheep whose pasture had been destroyed by frost.

Other news from the *Ross-shire* in January 1891 was the report that the Muir-of-Ord to Kilcoy section of the proposed railway through the Black Isle was going ahead. The following statement had appeared fifteen months earlier on 18th October 1889:

> *We understand that the Highland Railway Company have commanded the survey of a branch line from Muir-of-Ord to Fortrose and Cromarty.*

A week later an article had announced that it was to cost £65 000. The line as far as Fortrose, with stations in between at Redcastle, Allangrange, Munlochy and Avoch, was completed in 1894.

The February Communion holiday in 1891 was reduced to the Thursday only. However, not many children turned up for school on Friday. Were the God-fearing parents being defiant or did they think it was not worth sending their offspring to school for one day at the end of the week? Perhaps the absences were genuine: the following week's entry reported that attendance was low because the children were ill with colds.

In spite of the high absentee rate and the consequent poor progress, in March the top three standards (III, IV and V) 'commenced using Exercise books for Dictation and Story (Composition)'. This was a big step for the children who were used to erasing their work very quickly from slates. The Exercise books gave their work permanence.

Right through until July there were reports of bad weather, illness, and children being detained for farm work or for the market day. With so much absenteeism the teacher must have been very anxious about the annual inspection which took place on Monday 8th June. The report was received on July 1st.

The attendance is unduly irregular in some cases, more particularly in the case of one or two families residing in a district which has recently been added to the Parish.*

Under the new teacher the school has made fair progress, but there is still ample room for improvement. Better results would probably have been obtained if less had been attempted. In the present condition of the school, it would be well not to take up so many as three class subjects. Reading and Repetition are for the most part hurried, inaccurate and devoid of expression. Writing is careful as a rule, but a firmer and rounder style should be aimed at.

Arithmetic has improved.

The condition of the Junior Section of the school is not more than fair. Writing and figuring on slates require increased attention. Singing is very fair, but the testing exercises brought out rather poor results and only the lower grant can be recommended. Needlework is good. An earnest effort should be made to improve the discipline.

*Note: In May 1892 the areas of Muckernich, Bogroy and parts of Tore – all belonging to Allangrange Estate were officially transferred from the Parish of Knockbain to Killearnan by order of the Boundaries Commission.

In November sewing was taken in the morning because of the short day in the midwinter months. This was frequently mentioned over the years. Since small country schools tended not to have any artificial lighting until the nineteen twenties we can assume that in the 19th Century the children and teacher in Tore depended on daylight. Homes had oil lamps and candles.

In December the school was closed for a week, sanctioned by the School Board, to enable the teacher to attend the Christmas Examinations. We are not told what these were, but Miss Macdonald was probably enhancing her qualification.

The New Year holiday was given on 1st of January 1892 but the school was also closed during the week of the 15th because of stormy weather. Over several weeks there were comments regarding the poor attendance due to bad weather. There was a heavy fall of snow in mid-March. A young man who lived in Tore was married on the 18th of March to a girl from Kilmuir, near North Kessock. The ceremony took place in Drumsmittal School but before the bride could make her way to her wedding a snowplough (horse drawn) had to clear the road.

In Iowa, USA, the first petrol-powered tractor was built in 1892. This heralded the demise of horsedrawn equipment for agricultural work although, in the Black Isle, many years were to pass before the first tractor appeared.

Coincidentally, in the same year, a German engineer named Rudolf Diesel was granted a patent for his engine.

In school, sewing tests were given in April in addition to Arithmetic and Writing tests given the previous week. In the last two weeks of May attendance was poor because of the potato planting. The government examination (by Her Majesty's Inspector) was held on Monday 6th June with the following day given as a holiday. We can imagine how ill-prepared the children were for the Inspection having missed so many days of school.

The report on that visit recorded that there was,

> *an improvement in discipline and general tone of the school and the results brought out by the examination give evidence of faithful endeavour on the part of the teacher. Standard IV written work was weak. Counting was weak and 'fingering' was being used throughout the school.*

The habit of *'fingering'* (counting on fingers) was disapproved of by the Inspectors and usually discouraged by the teachers.

There has already been reference to children's absence because of the Muir-of-Ord market but Friday 29th July 1892 was given as a holiday because a number of the children were *'going to the Cattle Show in town'*. This event rather disparagingly called a Cattle Show was the Royal Highland Show which had begun on Tuesday 26th and was held in a field of Tomnahurich Farm. It had previously been held in Inverness in 1883.

A few days earlier on Saturday, 23rd July, the Black Isle Show had taken place at Rosehaugh. This seems to have been a sizeable event even in those days. (The last Black Isle Show before settling at its permanent site at Muir-of-Ord was held at Tore Mains.)

The school year ended with a Bible Exam and prizegiving but the teacher did not specify whether the prizes were just for Bible Knowledge. The children learned the Catechism, Metrical Psalms and portions of Scripture as well as stories from the Bible.

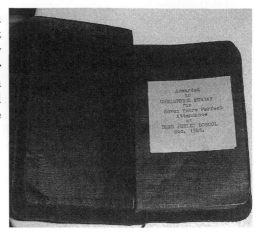

Bible given
for seven years perfect attendance
in 1941

Early Pupils

It was not customary for the teachers to name pupils in the Log Book but an HMI report on 22nd June 1892 made reference to two girls, Donaldina Paterson and Barbara MacDonald, who were due to leave school.

Donaldina (or Dolly as she was known) lived at Kilcoy. She was born in 1878, the sixth child of John Paterson and his wife May. The whole family spoke both Gaelic and English. Two older sisters and an older brother were among Tore School's first pupils in October 1879 and Dolly started school in 1883. Their father had a croft and also an inn where he provided refreshment for travellers on the road to Dingwall. We must remember that travel in the 1870s was on foot or horseback or by horse and machine. John, Dolly's brother, was known as Jock Hostie because of his father's hospitality as host of this inn. (Probably the father had the byname first.) The house where they lived had a thatched roof until the 1950s. In the twenties and thirties John's son, Tom, was a pupil of the school. In recent years, until his death in October 2004, Tom lived in a new house built only a few yards from the old family home.

In a rural community there was no great choice of employment. Boys might take up apprenticeships with local tradesmen – blacksmiths, joiners etc. – but were more likely to find employment as agricultural labourers or estate workers. For girls the attitude was that employment was just temporary, filling in the time until they got married. They might find work on farms but they were more likely to become domestic servants – possibly in the home of a member of the landed gentry or in a merchant's home. Where there were large families an older daughter might be required to help in her own home which of course brought in no income.

Dolly Paterson worked as a cook/domestic servant after she left school in 1892 and on 13th May 1897 she married George MacKenzie. He was a shoemaker and they made their first home in Jemimaville. They had a family of seven children. When they came to live in Tore they occupied a small wooden cottage which was situated in a fork where the roads from Muir-of-Ord and Dingwall met in the middle of the village. The cottage was demolished when the Muir-of-Ord road was diverted to form a T-junction. By this time the Mackenzies had moved across the road to Hill Cottage (now known as 'The Beeches'). Coincidentally, two further MacKenzie families occupied the cottage.

On the writer's earliest recollection of Mrs Mackenzie she must have been around seventy and was a widow. She was always called the 'Shoemaker's wife' to distinguish her from the three other Mrs Mackenzies in the village. There was the Smith's wife, the Shepherd's wife (by then living in the small wooden cottage) and the Stalker's wife (who lived in the croft – known as Tore Croft – at the end of the lane).

Dolly and George MacKenzie
top & below
their granddaughter
at the fork

It was customary, in the village, to gather sticks and pine cones (we called them duircean) for the fire. On a good day women from the village made an expedition with barrows and old prams and a retinue of children to the local wood. We'd spend all morning, and sometimes all afternoon, there. To us children it was great fun to gather sticks for the women to tie into bundles to be carried home later. Whenever I walk past the wood I think of Mrs MacKenzie and remember her with an armful of sticks, and a large bleeding scratch on her elbow. One of the little girls was very concerned about it but she shrugged it off as nothing.

One of the sons of Dolly and George MacKenzie, John, was killed in France during the First World War. He is buried in Terlincthun British Cemetery in France and his name appears on the War memorial at Fettes crossroads. Their other son, George, the only one to have attended Tore School, was evacuated from Dunkirk during World War II. Two of their daughters emigrated to America. Dolly herself died in 1956.

Four of her brothers, also former pupils of the school, went to Canada in 1904. Thomas came home but James, Colin and Hugh stayed and farmed in Saskatchewan. On his way home Thomas walked from Perth to the Black Isle. James served with Canadian forces in World War I and was a Prisoner of War at Cassell from 1917 to 1919.

Barbara MacDonald's father was a ploughman in Croftcrunie. She was born in Rosemarkie but some of her younger siblings were born in Avoch. They had lived in several different locations – which was usual for farm workers. None of that family was recorded as Gaelic speakers.

The cottages at Croftcrunie were not built until the 1900s. The son of a ploughman of the late 19th and early 20th Century wrote that his family had lived at Ryefield which was then part of Croftcrunie. It is likely that Barbara MacDonald's family had lived there previously. Barbara left school in 1892 but, unfortunately, we have no further information about her.

Another early pupil, Dolly Carr, was born in 1880 in Tore and was enrolled in Tore School from 1885. She, like the other two girls, would have been a pupil of Miss Jessie Forbes and of Miss Macdonald. When she left school she was one of several former pupils who emigrated to South Africa. She went there to join her aunt, Ann, to help her with her family. Dolly married William Whyte whom she met in South Africa and they had two children. Their home was in Port Elizabeth where Dolly died in 1958.

Her aunt, Ann Bain, was born in 1857 so was in her twenties by the time the Public School opened in 1879. The 1871 census entry indicates that she was a 'scholar' which means she was attending either the female school, or the Free Church School at Redcastle. On leaving school Ann worked as a nursemaid with a family which emigrated to South Africa taking her with them. In 1906 her son, James Knight born in 1895, was enrolled in Tore School while on a visit to Scotland with his mother.

1892-93

In 1893 New Zealand became the first country to give women the vote. That same year the slide (zip) fastener was exhibited in America.

The early part of the year was cold and stormy. The teacher recorded severe weather in January and February, and again in March when the school closed for two days because pupils could not attend.

In May a complaint was recorded from a parent regarding the water supply. It was noted that there was an abundant supply of water but that it would be an advantage to have a well or pump or gravitation from the spring above, fifty yards from the school. (On early maps a well is marked in the middle of the field behind the school.) There was a special meeting of the Board to deal with this problem and the result was a pump – completed eighteen months later in the week of December 14th, 1894.

1893 - 94

The weather in January 1894 was stormy. On the 26th the few pupils who attended school were sent home at the end of the morning.

In April the teacher entered in the Log Book that pupils were missing because of the potato planting. Sewing tests were carried out in May and the girls did *'pretty good on the whole'*.

The International Olympic Committee was formed in Paris in June 1894 and the first modern Olympic Games took place two years later.

Excessive rain on Friday 3rd August prevented many pupils from attending school. This was not an uncommon occurrence.

Allangrange Station   Photograph by J.L.Stevenson

The following Friday was a local holiday and the children were taken to Fortrose for a school trip. This appears to have marked the start of the summer holidays, the school reopening on 8th October. It is likely that they travelled by train because in February the railway line through the Black Isle from Muir-of-Ord to Fortrose had been opened. Allangrange Station was situated about half a mile from the school. The coalyard was on the site for many years, until recently, and there is little evidence left of the station. On the road the bridge over the railway is still obvious although the arch was filled in for safety reasons.

On Christmas Day 1894 the children were given an afternoon holiday but were back in school for the following three days. December 28th was a day of *'gales of wind and rain'* so the school did not open for the afternoon. From then until 7th January 1895 they had their New Year holidays but a severe snowstorm caused blocked roads so very few pupils attended on 7th January. Consequently the school was closed again until Monday 18th January but the roads were still bad and attendance was low.

The Day School Code that year introduced Drill into the curriculum and it began to be mentioned by the teachers in their notes in the Log Book. 'Drill' later became 'Gym' and is now known as 'Physical Education'.

Snow at the beginning of February caused Miss Macdonald to write in the Log Book, *'Attention specially given to the warmth and comfort of pupils while in School,'* and a week later, when attendance had improved, *'School kept warm. Frosty cold week.'* We can imagine the discomfort for the children in a room where there was no central heating and only one fire – with coal (or peat) burning and the teacher spending time keeping this fire well stoked.

March 15th had an interesting entry from a member of the School Board, *'Increased regularity prevails – pupils punctual and cleanly in appearance.'* There were, however, problems as indicated by the teacher's entry a week later. *'Many pupils do not prepare lessons except what is done in school.'* Her underlining conveys a sense of the frustration she was feeling regarding the children's attitude to Homework.

Although the holidays were not until August the school year finished on May 31st and the government examination was held on 3rd June. In his report received three weeks later the Inspector suggested,

> *With the view of securing a nearer approach to uniformity of size and style, the Board might consider the propriety of providing specially ruled slates for the younger children.*

The teacher was concentrating in July on certain aspects of the curriculum.

> *Due attention given to Scripture Knowledge, Drill and Singing in view of near approach of Prize Exam. Feel progress being made in different branches of knowledge – reading, writing and arithmetic.*

Then in August extra sewing and knitting were being done. The Exam took place on 21st August and Mr Trotter of the school Board described it.

> *A good number of the children's parents and others interested in school work were present. Miss Macdonald had an interesting*

programme which was gone through by all the children including Bible History and Catechism, vocal and piano music... A number of prizes were given to the children.

1895 - 96

Important events of 1895 included the discovery in November of X-rays by German Wilhelm Conrad Röntgen and in December the first public demonstration of the Cinématographe, the first motion-picture apparatus, invented by the Lumière brothers.

In the school the practice began (or was noted for the first time) of shortening dinnertime, to half an hour, and closing the school at 3.30 instead of 4 pm, from November, because of the short hours of daylight. This was to continue each year until the 1980s when 9 am became the opening time. Later references indicate that in the 19th and early 20th Century the morning began at 10 am. Because of the shorter dinner interval few children could go home so they took a 'piece' (packed lunch) to school and a bottle or flask of tea or cocoa which the teacher heated by the fire. The packed lunches would have been rather different to those of the present day. A 'piece' was bread and jam or dripping, or perhaps oatcakes and crowdie. Jam was homemade from the wild rasps and brambles which grew in the area.

Christmas had been receiving scant mention in the school Log Book until 1895 when Miss Macdonald recorded, *'On evening of 27th a Xmas tree entertainment was given on behalf of the pupils.'* We assume that until that time there were no parties at Christmas time.

On 10th April 1896 the teacher wrote, *'Great room for increased energy on the part of the pupils – in studying the lesson given.'*

The HMI report of the inspection on 10th July 1896:

> *The school has made marked progress during the year, and is now in a very satisfactory state of efficiency. Arithmetic is excellent throughout the percentage reached by the fourth and fifth standards being 87. Writing and figuring are also deserving of praise. The children answer very readily and intelligently in the oral examination Grammar and Geography. Needlework is very satisfactory. Grant £53.5.6d.*

There were notable events in 1896. Svante Arrhenis, in Sweden, predicted global warming (of which we hear much in this 21st century) and Becquerel discovered radioactivity. Marconi filed his patent for wireless radio. Can we imagine a world without radio? The first modern Olympic Games were held in April in Athens where they would return in 2004 for the 28th Games. In 1896 all two hundred and forty-one participating athletes were men.

The entry in the Log Book for December 25th 1896 indicated that the school closed that week for the Christmas and New Year holidays. An entertainment was held in school, pupils taking part in singing and recitations and the money raised by this effort was being kept for prizes for the children. Parents and friends attended, paying for the privilege – an early fund-raising event.

The beginning of 1897 was stormy and on Monday 1st and Tuesday 2nd February the school was closed because of a severe snowstorm.

In March Drill apparatus was supplied. The teacher recorded that the pupils took an active interest in the Drill lesson and that progress was good. There was a note dated 8th May to the effect that, *'Drill was given in the open air'* owing to the warm weather.

An epidemic of whooping cough, common in the days before vaccine, reduced attendance in May.

Queen Victoria celebrated her Diamond Jubilee on 20th June. We imagine the Victorians to have been patriotic to their Queen but there was no mention of any local celebration. In later years many royal events were marked by holidays. The Government examination took place on the 22nd (Tuesday) and the school was closed for the rest of the week. A holiday was customary after an Inspector's visit but did this year's also relate to the Jubilee?

In preparation for the *Prize Exam* the pupils were given some extra singing and Recitations and also Scripture lessons.

The school was examined on 17th August by Miss Macdonald in the presence of School Board members. They were *'entirely satisfied'*. The work was *'admirably executed'*. Prizes were given for Scripture Knowledge, attendance and good conduct generally.

1897 - 98

On December 10th the teacher recorded:

> *Great interest taken in home exercise work by Standard I pupils who are so pleased and proud to work sums in lead pencil or writing alternately.*

A week later she noted, *'duly received during the week "Scheme of the Ross and Cromarty County Committee Secondary Education".'* However, Tore was still not providing education beyond Elementary and older children were having to make the journey to Killearnan.

Epidemics – severe colds and measles – were prevalent in the early months of 1898 and one family was recorded with typhoid fever. In March the school closed for two weeks because of measles.

Thursday 11th August was a local holiday. The comment on August 12th is noteworthy. The attendance was low, *'owing to carelessness on the part of the parents not sending their children to school'*. On 17th August the school broke up for the summer holidays (six weeks). There were *'recitations and singing by the children and a number of prizes distributed to deserving scholars'*.

The annual Scripture exam, conducted by the ministers, had been held this year on a separate date – 10th August.

1898 - 99

In November word was received from the Clerk of the School Board that a monitor had been allowed to assist in the school. Annie Ellis was the person appointed and she began duty on 9th January 1899. Her role was similar to that of a pupil-teacher. At the end of 1899 the teacher recorded that Miss Ellis was *'absent with leave'* to revise for the Scholarship examination.

Miss Macdonald was not very pleased with the results of tests given at the beginning of February. A test in Arithmetic and written work was given to Standard II and upwards. A week later she wrote, *'Home preparation of lessons have not the attention that might be given to them.'* In May she recorded, *'Home Exercises begun and insisted upon.'* And by June she considered that the Home Exercises were very much improved.

In March the school was closed from 9th to 20th because of an outbreak of scarlet fever.

The June 9th entry recorded that drawing was begun – on slates. One of Her Majesty's Inspectors around this time had expressed doubts about the value of drawing in the curriculum. However, the entry on 2nd February of the following year indicated that drawing on slates was progressing with lessons twice a week and that the pupils seemed to enjoy the work. Later that year drawing books were supplied. This must have been more satisfying for the children instead of having to erase everything when it came to time for sums.

Daimler produced a new car in 1899 which he named after his daughter, Mercedes.

1899 - 1900

On 11th October 1899 war broke out in South Africa between the Boers and the British over sovereignty. It is likely that there were former pupils of the school involved in the fighting. Local men tended to join up with the Lovat Scouts or the Seaforth Highlanders.

The Black Isle District Committee donated the sum of 12s 6d during the last week of January 1900 to be given as prizes for the two pupils who were best at sewing. Although 12s 6d is equivalent to 62½p in today's money we have to remember that in 1900 it was more than half of a man's weekly wage. Flora Cameron won first prize and was awarded 7s 6d and Euphemia

MacLeod gained second place. Flora Cameron was about twelve years old and lived at Muckernich. By 1901 she was at home keeping house to her father who was a widower. Euphemia MacLeod lived at Crofthouse and was ten years old at the time of the award.

1899 Penny

February was a very stormy month with several closures, which included an extended Communion weekend holiday.

At the beginning of August one family was asked not to attend school because parents were objecting about whooping cough in the house.

Kilcoy Castle, original home of the Burton-MacKenzie family
on whose estate the school was built.

4. Into the Twentieth Century

1900-01

The new school year began on 10th October and many pupils, as usual, failed to turn up.

At the Martinmas term (November) Miss Macdonald recorded, *'Some new scholars admitted and some left the district.'* These would have been the children of farm workers who were moving to a new employer. Such movement of families created substantial fluctuation in school rolls.

In early December reference was made to sewing being taught earlier than the usual time of 3.15 to 4.15 pm. This was because of short hours of daylight, but what is significant is the late closing time of 4.15 pm.

On 25th December the school was closed but opened again from 26th until 28th when it closed at 2 pm. Classes were to resume again on the 4th of January 1901. As 1900 drew to a close, not only was a year ending but also a century. The 1st of January 1901 (not 1900) was considered to be the first day of the 20th Century. The *Ross-shire Journal* reported, *'The old century has gone out with a succession of storms.'* The events noted were no more than usual for Hogmanay – watchnight services in some Churches and a gathering on Dingwall High Street, where the band failed to turn up.

The Boers were continuing to fight the British in South Africa and Victoria was approaching sixty-four years as Queen. On 22nd January 1901 she died. It was a notable event but warranted no comment in the school Log Book. Her son was now King Edward VII.

At this time there were reputedly about ten thousand teachers in elementary schools in Scotland. Three thousand of them earned less than £75 per year and fewer than nine hundred earned over £100. The average salary for a woman teacher was £67.7.3d per year. Men were paid more.

A population census took place on 31st March 1901. The entry for Tore School was for Helen Macdonald, Teacher of Elementary School, and her sixteen- year-old sister, Isabella H. Macdonald. Miss Macdonald's place of birth was Dufftown in Banffshire; her sister's was Nairn. Neither of them spoke Gaelic. In 1901 less than half the population of Killearnan spoke Gaelic and most of those who did were adults. Very few children were Gaelic speakers.

In that year Marconi, using Morse Code, made the first transatlantic radio transmission. On 14th September the US President McKinley was assassinated. His successor was Theodore (Teddy) Roosevelt. In 1903 a child's toy was produced and called after him – the 'teddy bear'.

On 2nd August Miss Macdonald wrote:

No progress can be recorded as to home preparation of lessons. Pupils come, as a general rule with home written-work very carelessly done or not done. Attention given to secure better efforts on the part of the pupils.

Even in those days, it appears, children were not very enthusiastic about homework.

The holidays began on 16th August. Three days later Robert Trotter, a faithful member of the School Board, died at the age of fifty-six. He and his wife, who had died eight years earlier, are buried in Killearnan Churchyard. Mr Trotter had been a Justice of the Peace and a County Councillor.

1901 - 02

The school reopened after the summer break, on 1st October. On the 11th Miss Macdonald recorded that some pupils had left to attend Killearnan school. Tore School did not make special provision for children beyond the age of twelve and although some opted to remain some went to Killearnan where Post-primary courses were provided. (There is no mention until 1921 of pupils going to Dingwall Academy.)

Just five weeks after the school reopened Miss Macdonald sent her resignation to the School Board on 8th November. No reason was given. Miss McLeod and Miss I.H. Macdonald were *'accepted as substitutes until a Teacher is appointed'*. Was one of them Miss Macdonald's sister, Isabella? Their names were sent to the Scotch Education Department for approval.

That year for the whole of December the weather was stormy and roads were frequently blocked with drifting snow. The school closed early, or did not open at all, on several occasions throughout the month.

The stormy weather continued into January 1902. At the end of the month roads were blocked. Only eight children turned up so *'no school kept'*. Presumably the eight who did were sent home.

After three months Miss Helen Macdonald *'re-entered duty in this school on 17th February'*.

Jack Stables, a former pupil, writing to a member of the Tore staff in 1984 recounted how Miss Macdonald handled the whole school (over forty children) by herself but that the strap (tawse) was always in evidence.

There was still only one fire in the room – at one end. *'We knew what cold hands and feet meant.'* He also mentioned a card which hung above the fireplace giving the information that the capacity of the room was sixty-six children. That room was slightly larger than any of the present classrooms. According to an Inspector's comment, the children were seated facing the windows.

In April 1902 the Log Book contained a note to the effect that no Scripture lessons would be given until after the inspection. *'Nature Knowledge lessons are taken instead as these are behind.'*

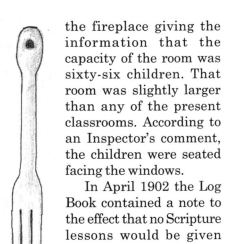

J. MacIver

A Tawse made by
J Dick of Lochgelly

There were several occasions over a number of years when this happened. A circular from the Scotch Education Department alleged that in many schools the year's work was done in the one or two months leading up to an Inspector's visit. This may well have been true when we consider the absenteeism during busy times in the farming world and when we read that Miss Macdonald concentrated on Nature lessons at the expense of Religious Instruction.

In spite of their Scripture lessons having been replaced by nature studies the report was favourable when, in August, Rev A. J. MacDonald conducted the Religious Knowledge examination. He wrote, *'This school is thoroughly well taught in Scripture Knowledge.'* Rev Aeneas MacDonald was the Church of Scotland minister from 1890 to 1932.

May 1902 marked the end of the war in South Africa when the Boers signed the Peace of Vereeniging thereby losing their independence.

The Coronation of Edward VII was scheduled to take place on 30th June but the King had to undergo emergency surgery for appendicitis and the Coronation was postponed until 9th August. On 15th July the school was closed in the afternoon. *'A coronation treat was given to the pupils at Redcastle by the Chairman of the School Board.'* At that time Tulloch McQueen, of Coulmore, was Chairman. We are not told where at Redcastle the treat was held but subsequent similar celebrations were held in a field in the Castle grounds.

1902-03

On December 15th 1902 the teacher noted that the school was closed because of diphtheria. This was a serious infectious disease which usually had fatal consequences but in the 1880s German scientists Edwin Klebs and Friedrich Löffler discovered the diphtheria bacillus and produced a vaccine. Immunisation meant that into the 20th Century occurrences of the disease were less common in this country. Protection of children became routine, usually during a baby's first few months.

The school did not reopen until the 7th of January 1903. During that first week the attendance was so low that classes finished each day – Wednesday, Thursday and Friday – at 2 pm.

In 1903 a Merit Certificate was replaced by the Qualifying Examination to determine whether a pupil in Standard 5 and aged about twelve went on to Supplementary Courses. This examination was the responsibility of the Scotch Education Department and was carried out by the Inspectors.

Even then Tore School did not offer Supplementary Courses so the older pupils went to Killearnan School.

The teacher wrote in the Log Book in February 1903 that more time was again being given to Nature Knowledge than to Religious Knowledge so a visit from the Inspector must have been looming. Perhaps Miss Macdonald preferred teaching Nature Studies. The inspection was not recorded but on 1st June a report was received in which the HMI suggested that the children could demonstrate a *'fuller and livelier style of answering'.*

Inventions of 1903 included the Electrocardiograph in the Netherlands. The Russian physicist Konstantin Tsiolkovsky advocated the use of liquid-fuelled rockets for space exploration.

In Britain Emmeline Pankhurst and the suffragette movement were fighting for the vote for women.

1903 - 04

'She ruled us by her gentleness.'

When the school reopened on 1st October 1903, after the long holidays, Miss Elsie Boyne began duty as assistant teacher. A nine-year-old of the time seemed to sense Miss Macdonald's less than positive attitude to the new member of staff. He wrote that Miss Macdonald did not take kindly to having an assistant. With a large number of children of different ages and abilities it was desirable to alleviate the burden but we must remember that in the absence of a second classroom the women had to share the one room. This may not appear to be a problem in an age when team-teaching is common but at the beginning of the 20th Century education was much more formal. With emphasis on learning by rote each teacher would be concerned to make sure that her pupils worked hard on this. We can imagine the noise as two sets of pupils chanted their memory work.

Miss Boyne has been described as *'a tall gentle lady. There was never any sign of a strap yet we became well mannered. We had an innate feeling of respect for her. She ruled us by her gentleness.'* Elsie Boyne was born in Nairn and in 1891 she was aged twenty. She had been a pupil teacher. By the time she arrived in Tore she was in her thirties.

While Miss Macdonald lived in the rooms at the west end of the school Miss Boyne lodged at Tore Inn. This was the building known (until recently) as Kilcoy Arms Hotel which was built in 1901. There was no schoolhouse as we know it today. It was built a few years later.

The first weeks of 1904 were very stormy and the school was closed early on several afternoons or did not open at all. HMI John Robertson carried out the annual inspection on 12th February in spite of bad weather. His report was received a month later.

> *Arithmetic poor, one Junior Class only one reading book. The teacher alleges much difficulty here, and in other classes, in getting full and prompt supply of Second Readers. The Board should see to this serious defect without delay. Wall illustrations are needed. Desks in poor condition because of adult meetings,*

three of which it is said take place weekly. The desks, of course,
were never constructed for the accommodation of adults.

When Inspector Robertson retired in 1905 he was presented with an illuminated testimonial containing the signatures of all teachers and several Board members in the areas where he had operated. Photographs of the staff and also of the school buildings and children accompanied many of the signatures. The book is about six inches (9cm) thick, fifteen inches (37cm) long and twelve inches (30cm) wide and bound in goatskin. James Forrest signed for Tore School but there was no photograph.

Mr Forrest

The handwriting in the School Log Book changed around the end of April 1904 and the next mention of staff included Mr James Forrest and Miss Boyne. In 1891 Forrest was schoolmaster in the School Board district of Crathie and Braemar. He was thirty-seven years old at that time. An unmarried sister lived with him and, according to the census, both were born in East Lothian. He designated himself, 'Class Certificated Teacher'.

Mr Forrest was straight-backed, whether walking or sitting, and he wore a double-breasted jacket. His beard was pointed and his speech was clipped. He put newspapers over the lower half of the window so that the pupils could see only the sky and the tops of the trees. Since, at that time, the road from Tore Mains passed outside the school there would be horses and machines going by – distracting to the pupils. Some of the boys would have preferred to be out there – herding cattle or sheep or on a farm gathering potatoes or bringing in the harvest.

A local man whose older siblings were pupils of Mr Forrest maintained that he was an excellent teacher. In his time the school roll increased greatly.

1904 - 05

Miss Boyne left just as the school opened in October 1904. Since there was no mention of a replacement for her we deduce that Mr Forrest then conducted the classes on his own. That first week an Inspector of Drawing visited.

A comment by the Clerk of the School Board dated 12th November 1904 reported:

> *a gratifying increase in attendance since the present teacher took charge and as there is now little room available for effective class movement, the managers will soon need to face an extension or re-arrangement of the premises.*

According to one of his pupils Mr Forrest was very ready to wield the strap. Pupils may, therefore, have been afraid to absent themselves without valid reason. The maximum number of pupils to be taught by a certificated teacher was seventy, soon to be reduced to sixty. For assistants the number was less. Can we imagine seventy children with one teacher today? The School Board Clerk's visit also prompted a comment on the inconvenience of the water supply. Ten years on the improvements of 1894 had become inadequate.

Mr Forrest wrote many remarks about the lack of knowledge among the children – a criticism of his predecessor. This, however, was a common practice with those early teachers, especially the men. He could also be critical of the School Board. In June, when the school roll stood at fifty, he commented,

> *the school is quite overcrowded and immediate steps should be taken to provide the necessary accommodation.*

After the usual Religious Knowledge examination took place in August Rev Aeneas MacDonald wrote in his report:

> *The school has made marked progress in Religious Knowledge under Mr Forrest – received greater attention than it has done for several years.*

This is not surprising since Miss Macdonald had frequently used the time for Nature Knowledge.

1905 - 06

We tend to think of children in early schools sitting still, very still, reading or writing and do not imagine them participating in practical mathematics. Perhaps Mr Forrest was ahead of his time when he suggested:

> *the managers might provide a cheap geographical globe and simple balances and examples of the common weights and measures for direct experimental use by the pupils.*

The year 1906 began and ended with severe snowstorms. On Friday 9th February attendance completely broke down owing to the snowstorm.

1906 - 07

In December 1906 Mr Forrest noted, *'Provision for additional accommodation is receiving the earnest attention of the managers.'*

A storm at the end of the year was even greater than at the beginning. The school closed two days earlier than planned for the New Year holiday.

Roads and railways were blocked and trains became stuck in snowdrifts.

At Achterneed
28th December 1906

Photograph by F W Urquhart

In April 1907 an Inspector's report referred to the teacher's interest in presenting a few pupils with a view to entering a Supplementary Class. Plans for improvements to accommodation should have been under way and the promise of more space would make this idea more attractive. It meant that future pupils would not face the long walk to Killearnan School.

For the three days, 13th to 15th May, the school was closed because of a death. Although Mr Forrest did not specify whose it was, we know from the inscription on the gravestone in Killearnan Churchyard that his mother died on Friday 10th May.

In that year the author Rudyard Kipling was the first Englishman to be awarded the Nobel Prize for literature. His 'Jungle Books' completed in 1895 were popular with generations of children.

1907-08

In his report received on 13th January 1908 the Inspector suggested that the managers supply copies of the official memoranda recently issued on the teaching of the leading subjects in the curriculum, and an up-to-date map of the world. He remarked that there was no improvement in accommodation. It was part of the Inspector's task to inspect all facilities and he found that the ashpit was uncovered – that was where the toilets were emptied – and the toilets themselves required proper seats.

One of the earliest cars, the Ford Company's Model T, went on sale and continued in production until 1927.

1908-09

Early in 1909 the weather was stormy and, as usual, attendance suffered.

Ernest Burton-MacKenzie, owner of Kilcoy estate, was at that time Chairman of the School Board. We gather that he lived at Belmaduthy although he also owned Kilcoy Castle. The other house owned by the MacKenzies – Tore Big House (or Castle) – had probably been demolished by then. (It was the one referred to by parents in the petition of the 1800s).

In June it was recorded that six pupils had applied for enrolment to the Supplementary Course.

Miss Christina Ann MacLennan began her duties as assistant teacher on 29th November, 1909. Since no alterations had yet been made to the building she and Forrest were, to begin with, teaching in one room. Miss MacLennan was the daughter of the schoolmaster in Conon School and in 1901 was aged seventeen and a pupil teacher.

Jack Stables

Rev Jack Stables, in his 1984 letter to Miss Margaret Buchanan, assistant teacher in Tore, supplied much information about the early years of the 20th Century in Tore School.

Although he was ninety years old when he wrote the letter he gave a remarkably clear picture of life in Tore School at that time. His father had been grieve in Croftcrunie. When he left school Jack worked in Hendersons in Dingwall but eventually went on to study to become a minister.

He worked for some time in Australia and in different charges in Scotland, his last charge being at Airlie in Angus. He was married to Betty Higgs but they had no family.

Mr Stables died in 1985, just months after he had written the letter to Miss Buchanan. The full text of this letter is printed in the book, 'KILLEARNAN The Story of the Parish' by Margaret Oag.

Ryefield with Croftcrunie fields beyond.
Croftcrunie Farm is on the extreme right.
In the background is Dunain Hill.

5. A New Georgian Age

On 6th May 1910 the King (Edward VII) died and was succeeded by his son, George V.

The school closed for Edward's funeral on 25th May.

1910-1911

After the summer holiday the school opened on 26th September but about half the pupils were absent because of the harvest.

The new accommodation was completed in 1910-11. His Majesty's Inspector's Report of March 1911 indicated that the

> *extension of the premises has contributed to improved efficiency.*
> *Junior pupils now accommodated in a separate classroom.*

Mr Forrest, with his customary economy of words, made little mention of that. Where there had originally been only one large room there was now also a smaller room. This must have been achieved by using the teacher's rooms. Generations of children, even after a major reconstruction in 1936, referred to the *wee room* and the *big room,* believing this to be a reference to the age of the pupils accommodated in each but probably, until 1936, it alluded to the room size. Today, with four rooms, three of which are usually occupied by classes, the same distinction is not likely. The schoolhouse was built shortly before the reconstruction, replacing the teacher's accommodation which became the smaller classroom.

Tore Schoolhouse

On the present school building there are two chimneys, each with two cans. Those on the west chimney would have been for the fires in the teacher's two rooms (open fires were the only means of heating at that time) while one of those on the east was for the classroom fire and later for the furnace which fed the central heating.

Photographs show that, until 1936, the building had tall narrow windows with large panes of glass. An entry in March 1911 in the accounts book of John Bain, carpenter, reads,

> *To the school Board of Killearnan parish:*
> *To one pane of glass fitted into window of Tore Public School.*
> *5 ft glass 3/6* (about 17½p)

Was it a snowball, a football or a stone? Nothing changes – except the size of the pane and the costs.

On 20th April the Medical officer visited the school. This was the first reported visit although Medical and Dental Inspections of school children were introduced in 1908.

Another event first mentioned in 1911 was the holiday for Empire Day on 26th May. This was also known (and still is in some places) as Victoria Day – it was to celebrate Queen Victoria's birthday.

On 16th June the record stated: *'A week's holiday in honour of the Coronation commenced today.'*

It was a very generous holiday to commemorate a one-day event and there was no mention of any celebration involving the children.

The grant received that year was £122.2.3d with the statement that,

> *The Managers should visit the school for the purpose of checking the register of attendances etc. not less frequently than once in every quarter.*

Management of attendance was one of the duties of the School Board and, although at times they were faithful in their task, there were periods when their supervision was not adequate. They seemed to turn a blind eye to the many absences for agricultural reasons which perhaps was not surprising since those of their number who were not farmers were likely to be working a croft.

1911 - 1912

In 1911 the government under Prime Minister Lloyd-George passed the National Insurance Act. Each employed person paid 4d per week and the employer's contribution was 3d. The government added a further 2d. This meant that workers were entitled to free medical attention and were guaranteed benefit for up to fifteen weeks per year if unemployed.

The school's HMI report received in March remarked that the Senior room had a good number of newcomers. For several years from 1910 the annual intake was over twenty ranging in age from four to thirteen. The biggest change was in November or May when the farm workers moved.

On 5th July 1912 the school was closed because of a measles epidemic. This was a serious illness in those days and there was no vaccination against it. Treatment was rest in bed with protection of the eyes and sometimes steam inhalations were given to relieve irritation in the bronchial tubes. It could be fatal but the mortality rate declined steadily in the 20th Century. In the 1960s the use of vaccine to protect against measles became widespread.

1912 - 13

The entry for 23rd September is intriguing – *'Mr Hood visited to inspect Cardboard work.'* Mr Hood was His Majesty's Inspector for Drawing so Cardboard work must have been something in the Art line.

On 12th February 1913 Miss Dawson, Messrs Hood and Morrison (all HMIs) visited the school. Miss Dawson was there to inspect sewing. The teachers must have been under pressure by the time HMI Macdonald examined the six pupils in the Qualifying Class on 18th July. The children in the Qualifying Class were aged eleven or twelve and this marked the end of their elementary education. Some moved on to another school while others proceeded to the Supplementary Class in the same school. A report on this visit was received in September.

> *The school is very fully staffed and well-equipped for the teaching of the ordinary branches of instruction in which good progress was made during the past session.*
> *It is pleasing to find that the selected pupils receive instruction in language – the boys in Latin and the girls in French.*
> *No provision, however, has yet been made for the practical instruction of the senior boys and girls. This is a matter of much regret inasmuch as the headmaster appears to be qualified to give instruction in Woodwork and his Assistant in Cookery. In view of the terms of article 72(b) of the Code it is earnestly hoped that this important matter will receive early and earnest attention and very particularly as the majority of pupils in the main room are beyond the Qualifying Class.*

The matter of practical instruction became a big issue. After an inspector's visit in 1914 there was a threat to reduce the grant if practical subjects were not taught.

World War 1

A former pupil in uniform

On 4th August 1914 Britain went to war with Germany. It seems unusual that there was no mention of this in the school Log Book. In fact there was no reference at all to the War although pupils whose fathers were called for service would have been affected by it.

People depended on a newspaper (the *Ross-shire Journal*) for information so from one week to the next most knew very little of what was happening and letters from those at the front could not contain much detail.

The summer holidays began on 14th August with what was described as *'the usual Exhibition'*. This was the first mention of an Exhibition. We might expect it to have been a display of work undertaken during the session.

However, the school year usually finished with the Religious Knowledge Examination and a programme of songs and recitations with parents present so it was more likely to have been this event. Did Mr Forrest have his own views on the children's performances?

The school reopened at the end of September, with fifty-seven children on the roll. There was then a week's holiday in October for the potato-lifting.

His father's diary recorded on 12th October that James Bain went to Redcastle School. He was born in 1901 so would have been thirteen at this time. Tore School was not providing practical work which may explain why parents continued to send their children to Killearnan. In 1923 James went to Canada where for a time he farmed in the prairies of Saskatchewan. Later, after he married, he moved to Victoria where family members still live. He died in 1968.

From 4th to 15th March 1915 the school was closed because of an outbreak of scarlet fever. Since whole families had to be isolated the attendance would be low and closing the school would restrict the spread of the illness.

In May Britain's worst train disaster took place near Gretna Green when two hundred and twenty-seven people, mainly soldiers, were killed.

Miss MacLennan left in June after working in the school for five and a half years and was replaced by Miss Duncan about whom little was written. Indeed, little was written in the Log Book between 1914 and 1918. Mr Forrest's comments were mostly about attendance and progress and these were very general. Miss MacLennan was teaching in Mulbuie School in the 1920s.

On 1st July 1916 thousands of British soldiers were killed on the first day of the Battle of the Somme.

1917-18

In 1917, at the end of October, the school closed for two weeks for 'potato holidays'. This made sense with so many children taking time off to help lift potatoes that school work suffered. During the war especially their help was essential since so many farm workers had joined the services.

The HMI report in December commented on the tidiness of the Headmaster's room but reprimanded the managers (School Board) for failure to certify the accuracy of particulars given in the registers. They had already received warning in a report in July. Consequently the grant was 'not readily awarded'. Visits from the School Board members at this time were very infrequent. They received a further warning in September 1918 concerning failure to make registration checks.

Nine children passed the Qualifying in April 1918 to move into the Supplementary Class.

In June Mr Forrest noted that eighteen children left at the term and only one had enrolled. This was a large depletion in numbers in the school. Those who left had been absent all of the previous week.

That year the responsibility for schools moved from the School Boards to elected Education Authorities, the majority of whose members had no specialist knowledge of schools. Teachers were excluded from these. However, School Management Committees which included parents and teachers were set up to look after the local situations but their powers were much less than of the Boards. The Scotch Education Department was renamed 'Scottish Education Department'.

At this time there was also discussion of raising the school leaving age to fifteen but it did not happen until 1945.

1918-19

Killearnan War Memorial, Fettes

At 11 am on the 11th of November 1918 World War I ended. This event was not recorded in the Log Book which seems strange considering the effect it must have had on the community. Former pupils were members of the forces fighting in that war but as far as is known none lost their lives.

Schools were closed on the afternoon of Wednesday 13th November because of the Peace Declaration and in 1919 an extra week of summer holiday was granted in celebration. None of this was mentioned by Mr Forrest.

He did record some shocking cases of absenteeism in late 1918.

15th November – Several pupils are seldom within the school door.
13th December – One girl returned after an absence of fifteen weeks. Her sister has made four attendances and her brother ten.

Many of the children were suffering from influenza. An epidemic in 1918-19 killed nearly thirty million people worldwide in six months.

In May 1919 seven schooldays were given for the potato planting. Later in that month (on the 19th) Miss Jessie MacKenzie took up the duties of Mrs Hutchison who had left on the 16th. There was no note of when Mrs Hutchison arrived at the school and it was unusual for a married woman to have an appointment. Miss MacKenzie was born in 1885 and grew up at Balgunloune.

6. The Twenties

Times were hard in the aftermath of the First World War. Many young people from this area, some of whom had fought in the War, emigrated to Canada and America.

This decade saw the development of flight and notably Charles Lindbergh's journey in May 1927 from New York to Paris – the first nonstop transatlantic flight – in thirty-three and a half hours. In the early twenties the wireless radio came into use although few homes were able to afford this luxury.

In 1920 a cartoon for children – Rupert Bear – appeared in the Daily Express and became a favourite.

Memories from the Twenties

Two residents supplied some reminiscences of the twenties.

My most vivid memory is of the poverty which came after the War. (World War I). People were desperately poor. I remember one day my mother had to go to Muir-of-Ord to pay bills. She didn't have a decent pair of shoes to put on but did find two (one from each of two different pairs) and she went wearing these. She had to cycle there.

The school (Ferintosh) seemed to be full of boarded-out children. They were fostered by crofters. I think that's the only way some crofters could survive – with the money they received from fostering the children. And the children would help them on the croft. Crates of clothes for the Glasgow children arrived twice a year. They were lovely clothes. My father was a cattleman but he earned so little that we couldn't afford nice clothes. Those we had were handed down. I started work as a domestic servant at fifteen.

****

I was five when the twenties began. I can remember the children on the donkey cart going for wood. When the sawmillers moved away from Broomhill we used to dig in the sawdust (with our bare hands) to find the slabs (wood) buried there. Most weeks, when I was a bit older, I cycled to Avoch to sell eggs and the crowdie and butter which my mother had made. (No food hygiene regulations then.)

At dinnertime in school the boys liked to go to the Moss (the wood along the ridge) for gulls' eggs. What a fright we got the day my pal, Ack, fell in the loch. I grabbed a long stick and pushed it out to him and he hung on.

Ack (Alec Paterson) must have had an uncomfortable afternoon. We are sure he did not go home to change his clothes.

A child of the thirties remembers the big boys returning to school with the gulls' eggs and eating them raw!

Artist's impression of a 1920s schoolroom

J. MacIver

In April 1920 Donald MacLeod began work as Headteacher in the school. The very morning he started the school was inspected by two of His Majesty's Inspectors. Just over a week after this he wrote in the school Log Book,

> *The school is outstandingly poor in equipment; there is not even a blackboard in the Senior room, a piece of battered brown canvas about a square yard in extent having to be utilised in place of a proper board – a rather inconvenient and imperfect substitute. The supply of school material in use – nothing in stock – is uncommonly meagre: several children have no readers of any description; no textbooks in Arithmetic. There are no exercise books, no slate pencils; and about half the slates are cracked; but there is an abundance of chalk.*
>
> *There is a ragged remnant of a school library (Coats); enough to fill three shelves out of the twelve fitted into the book-case in which the volumes were originally housed.*

Immediately after this note the following was inserted: *'and in 1927 when your successor took over there was nothing left at all.'*

J. P. Coats was a textile manufacturing company in Paisley and generous to schools. They donated books for libraries and in 1914 had provided all school children with a leather schoolbag.

The first reference to school holidays for Easter was in 1920 when a letter was received on 16th April, from the Clerk of the local School Management Committee, Mr W. Campbell. All schools which had not closed for Easter were advised to close for a week at the earliest possible date. Tore School took the holiday from 30th April until 9th May .

On Saturday 12th June applicants for an Intermediate Bursary attended a Control Examination set by the County Education Authority from 10 am to 12 noon. Thirteen applicants from Mulbuie, Killearnan, Tore and Arpafeelie were present. There is no record of how these young people fared and whether any were successful in gaining a bursary to take them to Dingwall Academy.

On 22nd July 1920 the annual Religious Knowledge examination was conducted by Rev Aeneas MacDonald and the prizes were given by Thomas MacDonald, Croftcrunie, who represented the district on the Education Authority.

It is interesting to note that Thomas MacDonald's children attended a private school set up by Mr Forrest after he had retired in 1920 as Headmaster of Tore School. This was held in a wooden building at the back of his house (also wooden) less than a hundred yards from the Public School. He was assisted by his niece, Mrs Polson. Forrest died in 1936 at the age of eighty-three and is buried in Killearnan Churchyard.

James Forrest's grave
in Killearnan Churchyard

Mrs Polson lived on in the house and was a well-known figure into the 1950s. When she died the house was sold and demolished so that a new house could be built on the site. This house is still known as Woodneuk.

1920-21

The new school session began on 1st September and on 13th September Dr Leitch, Beauly, vaccinated all Glasgow Parish Council children who were present. Because of an outbreak of smallpox in Fortrose all children in the school were then vaccinated or revaccinated. One man who was in the Infant class at the time remembered children fainting during the vaccination. The Headmaster wrote in the Log Book that three, all from the same family, had fainted. School closed in the afternoon but from then on until well into October attendance was poor because children were suffering from the effects of the vaccination.

On 26th October after instruction from the School Management Committee, and in consultation with Mr MacDonald, Croftcrunie, the school closed for a week for *'potato holidays'*.

In November a meeting of the local School Management Committee set the date for the Christmas and New Year holidays – to close on Friday 24th December and open on 4th January.

His Majesty's Inspector visited on 16th December and the report of this inspection was received on 12th January 1921.

In both rooms satisfactory work is being done in most subjects. In the upper classes the logical arrangement of answers to arithmetical questions deserves favourable mention; but in oral subjects answers should be fuller and more pointed. Class Junior I did well in all the subjects tested.

It is unfortunate that there is no provision in the school for practical instruction. Practical work for the older scholars is very desirable, and in the present instance the pupils of the senior classes are nearly all too old for their stage of advancement. The Education Authority are recommended to make the necessary provision at an early date.

Pail closets have recently been introduced, and the walls of the classrooms were distempered during the summer vacation. These are very gratifying improvements.

Although children in Tore had been undergoing medical inspections from 1911, an entry on 11th January 1921 contained the first specific information. Dr Brodie visited the school and examined children in the following categories:

    a. those admitted since his last visit

    b. those due to leave before the end of the present school year

    c. pupils of ages nine and eleven

    d. special cases.

On 12th January he granted certificates excluding three pupils from attending for periods ranging from four to seven days. The reason was not recorded but may have been ringworm, impetigo or 'dirty' heads.

During the week of 4th February the only absentee was one boy on Thursday afternoon. This must have been a record – good attendance was not a characteristic of this school.

An overnight snowstorm reduced attendance on 2nd March, especially among the younger pupils, to much less than half. After some beautiful weather in April there was further snow in May. By this time of year fires would probably not be lit but during the week of 9th May they were necessary in both rooms every day.

1920/21

Back Row: L to R __, __, Hugh MacLennan, Duncan MacLennan, __, __.
2nd Row: ? Paterson, __, __, __, __, __.
3rd Row: Mr D. MacLeod, David Bain, __, __, Mary Bain, __, __, __, Miss Jessie Mackenzie
4th Row: __, __, __, Chrissie MacLennan, Margaret MacLennan, ? Paterson, __, Dolly Bain
Front Row: Nancy MacKenzie, __, ? Forsyth, __, __, __, __, Donald Bain, Walter Matheson, __.

The Control Exam took place on 13th June. There were five children from Mulbuie, four from Killearnan, three from Tore and two from Arpafeelie, supervised by teachers from each school.

1921 - 22

The summer holidays ended when the school opened on 30th August but a large number of pupils were absent.

> *Mary MacKenzie and Mary A. Bain – pupils in the Supplementary class of the school – have been granted an Intermediate Bursary by the Education Authority and have entered the Higher grade Department of Dingwall Academy.*

Those girls travelled by train from Allangrange Station to Muir-of-Ord where they changed and joined the Dingwall train. From the station in Dingwall it was a short walk to the Academy on Tulloch Street. The new building on the hill was not opened until 1939.

Mary Bain and friend
at Dingwall Station

Mary MacKenzie lived with relatives at Tore Croft, down the lane, at the back of the village. Sadly she developed tuberculosis and died in January 1923 at the age of fifteen.

Mary Bain's father was a carpenter in the village, where her younger brother, Donald, lived until his death in August 2004. When she was fifteen years old Mary emigrated to Canada where several brothers and a sister had already settled. In Montreal she worked in domestic service and married in 1928. She had one son who still lives in Montreal. She died in 1994 at the age of eighty-six.

When Arpafeelie School was downgraded to one teacher in August 1921 ten children, all over ten years of age, were transferred to Tore.

Margaret Ann MacLean (Mrs Hutcheson, Artafallie) was one of those pupils and was in her final year of school. Along with several other children she walked from Glaickmore, on a route which then went through the village. One little boy of the time remembered her taking part in a snowball fight there on the way home from school. At the time of writing she was the oldest former pupil still alive.

On 7th September 1921 a meeting of the British Cabinet took place in Inverness Town House. This was the only time the Cabinet ever met outside

London. The Prime Minister, Lloyd-George, was having a break in Wester Ross when he received word that Ireland had rejected the King and the Empire. The King was on holiday locally as was the Depute Prime Minister.

One month into the session the school books and materials were ordered. They took five weeks to arrive.

In October/November there was an epidemic of whooping cough. At that time there were no vaccinations against this distressing illness.

For the first time, on Armistice Day (11th November) 1921, poppies were worn in remembrance of those who had died in the War. They were made in the Earl Haig workshops, the poppy being symbolic because of those which grew in the fields of Flanders where many soldiers died.

Visitors to the school included Dr George Philip who was Executive Officer for the County Council (and a fairly regular visitor) and Dr Brodie who arrived to inspect a girl *'who was reported as being verminous'*. He gave a lecture to the girls *'on cleanliness of body'*.

When the school reopened on 3rd January 1922 after the Christmas and New Year holidays the teacher wrote,

> *Only sixteen pupils present on account of the severity of weather. Throughout the whole of the holiday period now ended the weather was exceptionally severe with high gales, heavy rain, sleet and snow alternating and intermingling, so that it was only a favourable coincidence for the children that the school was closed.* (Did the children agree?)*The ground today is coated with snow and as the great majority of the children live a considerable distance from the school only a few could reasonably be expected to attend.*

The weather continued cold and wintry for the next two weeks. Mr MacLeod gave some vivid descriptions of what was happening.

> *Jan 16th Snow has been falling without intermission since dusk yesterday and the ground is evenly covered with a beautiful coat of dry flaky snow, several inches in thickness; the attendance at school is better than one would expect – 64 per cent of the number on the roll.*
>
> *Jan 17th (2pm) It is still snowing without a break from the evening of the 15th, and the ground is coated with a smooth layer of snow to the depth of a foot or so; fewer children in consequence faced the school journey today – 46 per cent.*
>
> *Jan 18th The fall of snow ceased yesterday afternoon some-time between 2 and 4 o'clock; but today there is a fairly strong breeze of very cold wind blowing, and this, along with the partially-blocked pathways kept the farther-away children at home – 51 per cent present.*

Jan 19th A gentle thaw set in yesterday morning, and today the roads are somewhat slushy.

On Friday there was no dinner hour and pupils were dismissed at 2 pm. On instructions from the school Management Committee the school was closed on 28th February in honour of the marriage of Princess Mary. She was the only daughter of King George V and aunt of the present Queen.

In the election of the County Education Authority on 7th April Mr MacLeod acted as Polling Clerk for the Parish, the election being held in Killearnan School which was closed to pupils for the day. In his absence his wife, Katherine, who was also a certificated teacher took his classes in Tore.

Attendance continued to be affected annually because of farm work. In June 1922 Mr MacLeod wrote: *'Drop in attendance ....detained at home to help with work either in house or field.'*

Rev Aeneas J. MacDonald and Rev A. Cameron, the United Free Church minister, carried out the Religious Knowledge examination. The following day the school closed for the summer holidays after prizes donated by the Education Authority were presented.

On 29th August, the day on which the school opened again, the Religious Instruction report, signed by Aeneas MacDonald, was copied into the Log Book.

In both divisions the appearance made by the pupils was highly creditable; I only wish that the Chairman of the Authority or His Majesty's Inspector had been present to witness it. Great credit is due to the teachers in school for the thoroughness with which religious instruction is given; their hearts are clearly in this work.

One former pupil expressed the opinion that, since the teacher usually did the questioning, he was sure to ask the children who would know the answers.

1922 - 23

During the summer holidays the ceiling and woodwork on the walls of the senior room and the whole interior of the lobby was varnished and all the outside woodwork of the building painted. This was the first report of decoration since the reconstruction of the building twelve years earlier.

For about six weeks in November and December 1922 the assistant teacher, Miss MacKenzie, was absent suffering from eye trouble. In the mornings from 10 am to 1 pm the master taught all the classes himself. In the afternoon his wife, Katherine, took Miss MacKenzie's classes. The MacLeods had four daughters, Anna, Isabel, Catriona and Donalda, the eldest of whom must have been about seven years old at this time, which probably explains why Mrs MacLeod could not cover classes all day. The last known whereabouts of Mr MacLeod's daughters was Stirling.

The Inspector refers to Miss MacKenzie's absence in his report which was received in the school on 5th January 1923.

During the past six weeks the conducting of the school has devolved upon the headmaster owing to illness and consequent absence of the assistant teacher and the various classes were seen at a disadvantage. Notwithstanding the standard of proficiency at the different stages remains creditable.

In the report on the visit paid to the school on 16th December 1920 the absence of provision for instruction in practical work was criticised. The attention of the Education Authority is again directed to the great desirability of incorporating in the curriculum some form of practical work for the older scholars: it is hoped that steps will be taken at an early date to make the necessary provision.

There was also reference to the *'offices'* (toilets) which were dirty and had not been cleaned *'for a considerable time'*. It was noted in the Killearnan Log Book that a person was appointed there for the task of emptying the pails. In Tore it was not stated who was responsible – possibly the Headmaster.

Miss Jessie MacKenzie who had been assistant teacher in the school for four years resigned on 31st December and in February 1923 she married William Macdonald from Beauly where they subsequently made their home. The wedding took place at the Caledonian Hotel, Inverness. In March the children presented her with a silver cake stand and she entertained them *'to a service of tea and cakes'*. Sadly, Jessie Macdonald died four years later in April 1927 at the age of forty-one.

Miss MacKenzie was replaced, in January 1923, by Miss Jessie MacGregor who belonged to Dalwhinnnie. She had recently trained in Edinburgh and was just twenty-two years old when she started work in Tore. She lived in a small house, The Bungalow, which was attached to Furness House and rented out by the owner.

One former pupil told about being taken by Miss MacGregor to Allangrange WRI, meeting in Arpafeelie School, where he sang a solo.

The master recorded on 23rd April the intimation that:

it is the desire of His Majesty the King that a holiday should be granted to children in the schools in Scotland on the 26th inst., being the occasion of the marriage of His Royal Highness the Duke of York.

This request was duly carried out. The Duke of York, who later became King George VI, married Lady Elizabeth Bowes-Lyon. They became the parents of the present Queen. When King George died his wife became known as the Queen Mother. She died in 2002 at the age of a hundred and one.

On 4th May Nurse Chisholm *'examined all pupils as to cleanliness of person and clothing'*. This is the first mention of such an inspection but it became a regular feature. Three days later – probably as a follow-up to the Nurse's visit – Dr Brodie called and isolated two pupils with impetigo and two were instructed to get their hair cleaned. They were given written instructions to take home. Brodie also noted that the *'offices'* were filthy and he was sending a report direct to the Executive Officer. Two days later Brodie and Philip (Executive Officer) visited the school. Nurse Chisholm returned to the school on 26th June and *'looked at several children to note progress in cleanliness'*. A few days later a further three pupils were isolated by Brodie – because of impetigo.

On 10th May there was sleet and snow and two hours after the fire had been lit (at 8 o'clock in the morning) the temperature had reached only 42°.

On 31st May the following entry was made: *'Mr D. MacKinnon has erected a door – complete with lock and key – to the enterance (sic) to the urinal and boys' closet.'*

Mr MacKinnon was one of the local carpenters. Was this piece of work done to ensure the privacy of the pupils or to stop the place being used by the public at night?

1923 - 24

In August 1923 Christina Jane MacKintosh, who was thirteen at the time, was granted an Intermediate Bursary by the Education Authority and entered Dingwall Academy. About two weeks later Robert Clark followed her. There had been a misunderstanding over his award so he was later in going on to Secondary School.

Christina lived at Broomhill and had come to Tore School from Arpafeelie in 1921. She was one of the many former pupils who emigrated: she went to South Africa.

From 1923 to1936 the Supplementary Courses were known as 'Advanced Divisions' and provided general and vocational courses. Some of the literature read and studied in these senior classes was serious and included poetry. In 1924 the promotion examination ceased to be conducted by the Inspector and became a written exam in English and Arithmetic and in some counties became known as the Promotion Examination. In Ross-shire it retained the name 'Qualifying' or 'Qualy' as the candidates called it.

It is significant that among the circulars coming in the autumn from the Education Authority were two concerning potato lifting – one for teachers and one for farmers. Much attention seems to have been given to improving attendance and to cutting down on the absences caused by children being kept off school for farm work. It was recorded that offenders had been reported to the Education Department. The granting of days of holiday for potato-lifting appeared to be an attempt to reduce the disruption to lessons.

In early 1924 the weather was very stormy. Mr MacLeod wrote graphically about this.

February 29 The greater part of this week has been rather wintry but the attendance until today has been much about the usual. Today we have Arctic weather – heavy and frequent spells of snow accompanied by high winds which drive the snow about in spindrift. Very few of the Infant and Junior children came to school.

March 3 The snowstorm which began on Friday morning about the time children would be on their way to school gradually increased in violence until by the early evening a regular blizzard from the North and North-west was raging: it continued with unabated severity for more than twenty-four hours. Main roads, side roads, and all paths are blocked with huge wreaths of snow so that the attempt to walk a few miles even – in any direction – today is a task for which only the strongest and sturdiest of grown-ups are fit.

Fifteen children came to school: all these with the exception of one boy, who is much above the average in physical equipment, are within easy reach of the school.

For the following three days the bad weather continued but a thaw set in on the 7th of March. The attendance, however, improved little until after the weekend.

A local resident who grew up in a neighbouring parish, and was eleven years old then, said:

I remember that snowstorm. Our school (Ferintosh) was closed for the Communion weekend. We had 'flu and we were supposed to be in bed but we kept getting up to see what was happening. I remember two cars were stuck near the house.

A former pupil who lived in the village wrote:

We didn't have far to go so I would have been in school. But I remember about the MacKenzies in the little wooden house at the junction: they kept thinking it was still night time but wondering why it wasn't getting light. Eventually they got up. The snow had drifted against the windows.

School Garden

In spite of the severe weather a start was made in March to meet the Inspectors' demands that there should be practical work for the older pupils. This entry for 28th March 1924 gives an indication of the task ahead for the master and his pupils.

> *Commenced practical instruction in School Gardening on the second week of this month. A portion of the playground has been set apart to be made into a garden. The selected plot is exceptionally hard and stony and the quality of the little soil there is, is poor, and to trench it to a depth of even two feet is a work requiring considerable physical strength; and worse still, on account of the absolutely flat position of the area, the land is water-logged. The eastern section of the patch is covered with heather and whins. In the past three weeks we have cut the whins, removed turf from the whole plot, dug many stones – one weighing several hundredweights – and dug one trench.*

On 1st May Dr Philip, the Executive Officer, suggested that because of the expense involved draining of the plot should be left until the following year. However, on 9th May there were plans to trench the ground but because the garden was sodden nothing was done that day. Trenches which had been left open were full to the brim. It was not a good start.

The garden was situated in the corner to the north-east of the school and the descriptions give us an idea of what this area must have looked like in the 1920s. One pupil remembered  that they each had their own patch in the garden.

A 1980s picture of the corner where the garden had been sited.

In October 1928 Mr MacLeod's successor reported that he had discussion with His Majesty's Inspector regarding the school garden and had thoughts of abandoning the experiment.

> *There is no wind protection and any crop that survived the inroads of rabbits was broken by the winds. The soil is rank and lacks humus.*

The year 1924 saw the first Labour Government elected into power when Ramsay MacDonald became Prime Minister. He belonged to Lossiemouth.

1924 - 25

At the beginning of 1925 the Headmaster was granted leave of absence for a few weeks. Miss Nicholson from Fodderty was appointed to act as Headteacher and to take the Advanced and Supplementary classes. She shared the house known as 'The Bungalow' with Miss MacGregor and a former pupil from the village remembered them out with bikes on the road practising (or attempting) 'tricks'.

It wasn't just snow which disrupted education. In July there was such heavy rain that *'the children were soaked to the skin on way to school. The children were detained over dinnertime and school closed early.'*

1925 - 26

The Headmaster was again absent from September until December when Miss C. F. Mackenzie took charge. During this time Miss MacGregor was working as assistant teacher in Killearnan School.

On 22nd September the school was visited *'by a gentleman who was a pupil here fifty-two years ago. He addressed the children very shortly and left a school fund to provide four special prizes for the four best writers according to ages and stages.'*

Since the Public School did not open until 1879 this man must have attended, as a small boy, the female school which was on the site prior to that. It is a pity that Miss MacKenzie did not record this man's name.

Following adverse comments in the HMI report in September regarding the lack of Science in the Advanced Division, the subject was added to the curriculum from Monday 10th November. The school day was opened for the Advanced Division at 9 am to fulfil the demands of an extra subject.

An entry for 27th November highlighted the dangers to children involved in farmwork. A girl was recorded as having been absent for four and a half weeks because she had caught and crushed her hand in the threshing mill. She was not named in the report.

In 1926 US rocket pioneer Robert Goddard tested the first liquid-fuelled rocket.

A. A. Milne published his first book about the lovable bear, Winnie the Pooh, a character who was to delight children for many generations and who remains as popular today as he was all those years ago.

In February 1926 there was a flu epidemic. The teacher recorded that attendance was sixty-six per cent and that those present were *'not in a very radiant condition'.* On May 7th he wrote:

> *We have had the best attendance of the year this week – except for the opening week of the session. From Jan. 15 to Ap. 30 the weekly average did not on a single occasion reach 90 per*

cent of the number on the roll. There has been an extraordinary amount of illness amongst the children throughout the winter and spring. This has been the first week for at least six months that no cases of sickness have been reported amongst the children; and it is to be hoped that this state of general physical efficiency shall prevail for the rest of the year.

Three days later, 10th May, Mr MacLeod's entry in the Log Book read:

Climax and anti-climax! The rosy optimism of the last entry has not continued long. The splendid attendance of last week, after such a long period of recurrent illnesses – epidemic and spasmodic – had naturally raised expectations of a summer session of robust physical and mental activity; but these fond anticipations have already been suddenly and rudely dispelled, for, this morning twenty-one children are absent, and all these – except two (who may also be ill) are reported to be unable to attend school because they are sick. Of the twenty-one who are absent, twenty were present on Friday, so that the wave of sickness has been sudden and strong; children from every part of the school district are affected.

During the month of June there were several cases of German measles among the pupils, prolonging the reduced attendance.

1926-27

In September 1926 Mr MacLeod left to take up an appointment at Breasclete School (in Lewis). Mr MacLeod was a Gaelic speaker and one of his former pupils in Tore remembered him teaching them Gaelic songs to perform before parents and friends – probably at the soirée.

Miss M. E. Napier was appointed to Tore and Miss MacGregor was to act as Headteacher *'during the interregnum and to continue in charge of the Infant and Junior Departments'.*

On 1st October Miss Davidson visited the school and took the children out for Drill.

A visit from HMI Mr J. Watson later in the month led to the establishment of a ten-minute interval during the forenoon.

Disruption occurred at the end of October when parents refused to send their children to school because there was no fire in the Junior classroom as a result of a broken grate. It was mended within a short time and on 11th November Mr Matheson, Architect, called to check it.

The report of His Majesty's Inspector of 22nd October indicated a school roll of seventy-four children.

*The Junior room which has accommodation for 33, has 39
pupils and the senior room with accommodation for 40 has 35
pupils. (Signed by J Watson.)*

Whether as a result of the HMI visit or a call from Dr Philip a third
teacher was appointed – Miss Janetta MacLennan from Evanton. She was
to take the children of Classes 3 and 4 and Miss Napier would have the
Qualifying and Advanced classes. Since there were only two classrooms for
three teachers these two must have shared the big classroom.

Miss MacLennan is fondly remembered by many of her former pupils.

New Year, New Master

On 4th January 1927 Angus Murray, previously of Sheildaig Primary School,
took up his duties as Headmaster.

He seems to have come with determination to improve the school. One of
his first tasks was to compile a list of pupils *'according to ages etc'* to see
where rearrangement could be made. Presumably he was concerned about
the overcrowding and the large numbers in the smaller room.

On 23rd February it was recorded that work was done on the school
garden. On 29th April snow caused the destruction of the crop. That day the
school closed at 1 pm because of the snow.

Photograph: Scholastic Souvenir Company

Football Team 1927

Back Row:- Jeff MacKay, Jimmy MacKenzie, Jimmy Sutherland, John Black, Donald Bain, John Fraser.
Front Row:- Callum MacAskill, Alister Lumsden, Donald Sutherland, Walter Matheson, Frankie Black,
Jim Forsyth.

Photograph: Scholastic Souvenir Company

1927/28

Back Row: Alastair MacLennan, Alec Paterson, __, Rob MacKay, James Forsyth, Alec Sutherland, Finlay MacLennan, Miss MacGregor.
2nd Row: __, Roddy Macleod, Joey MacKenzie, Betty Gammie, Cathie Johnstone, Barbara Johnstone, Agnes Forsyth, Frances Cameron, Alfred Park, Archie Kirk.
3rd Row: __, Marion MacKenzie, Pearl Harper, __, Janet Park, Madda Fraser, Molly Forsyth, Chrissie Sutherland, Agnes MacKenzie, __, Cathie MacRae.
Front Row: __, Murdo Matheson, Donnie Kirk, Hamish?, Tommy Paterson, Fraser Stewart, Adam Forsyth, __, Frankie Black, __.

1927-28

On 30th August 1927 Miss Cecilia Murray (no relation to the Headmaster) began three weeks of teaching practice at the school. Miss Murray lived at Allangrange Station where her father was stationmaster. Her sister was a pupil in Tore School but she herself had completed Elementary education before the family moved to Tore.

HMI Watson inspected the school on 5th September and the Headmaster noted that he was satisfied with the Chambers series of readers. These seemed to have been newly introduced.

Mr Murray recorded, on 7th October, that he was not satisfied that the School Management Committee was making an effort concerning attendance and had sent a letter to them. This may have arisen because the potato-lifting would be going on around this time. On 14th October he received a letter from the Clerk of the Management Committee. He took the opportunity to interview the Clerk 'as a more speedy and satisfactory way of settling matters'. We are not told how those matters were settled.

In November Miss Davidson, the Drill teacher, caused disruption by taking the children at different times from those scheduled. There was, as yet, no public hall in the community and the school had two very full classrooms so Drill was taken outside if at all possible. This was winter-time and the days were short. By the late 1920s Tilley lamps (pressurised paraffin lamps) were in widespread use so indoors the failing light did not present the problems of an earlier age.

On 25th November Rev Dr Dow who was a member of the Education Authority called in the morning and Dr Brodie and Dr Philip arrived at 3.50 pm. The two afternoon visitors examined the registers with a view to sending some children to other schools to relieve the accommodation problem. For over a year there had been two teachers in the one room. Three of the worst attenders were removed – but we are not told where they went. On 4th January, 1928, after the Christmas holidays,

Seven pupils from Redcastle Station and four from Newton of Ferintosh moved to Killearnan and Mulbuie respectively on account of the numbers in Tore being considered too high for the available accommodation.

The Killearnan School Log Book contained a note that five boys and two girls from Tore School enrolled. Some of the children described as *from Redcastle Station* were in fact from Kilcoy.

In 1928 the Morris Minor car went on sale. It became so popular and reliable that it was to last into the 1970s.

Alexander Fleming discovered penicillin in the same year.

On 25th January Miss Davidson observed the Headmaster taking his own class outside. The ground was considered entirely unsuitable and the Infant and Junior classes were not allowed out. From the records it would appear that the Drill teacher visited every alternate month.

Mr Murray expressed a complaint on Monday 30th April that the floors were: *'dirty and untidy – people eating sweets in religious service. Forms not replaced'.*

1928 halfpenny

Every Sunday evening this Church service was held and the Ministers of the three local Churches – Parish Church, Free Church and United Free Church – took turns of conducting it. Many local people attended, regardless of their denominational affiliation. When the Public Hall was opened, in the thirties, the services then took place there. By that time the United Free Church had amalgamated with the Church of Scotland.

The summer holidays began on 12th July and ended on 4th September. On 26th October the school closed for a week for potato holidays but this was not sufficient for the farmers and crofters to complete the tattie-lifting. Prior to the holiday there had been poor attendance because children were helping with the harvest.

1928/29

Photograph: Scholastic Souvenir Company

Back Row: Miss MacGregor, Mr Murray, Miss MacLennan.
2nd Row: Fraser Stewart, Adam Forsyth, __, Roddie MacLeod, Alastair MacLennan, James Forsyth, __, Alec Paterson, Archie Kirk, Finlay MacLennan.
3rd Row:Janet Park, Chrissie Sutherland, Agnes MacKenzie, Frances Cameron, Agnes Forsyth,Betty Gammie, May Hynie, Barbara Johnstone, Peedie Cameron, Madda Fraser, Cathie MacRae, Cathie Johnstone.
4th Row: Mary Murray, __, __. Lily Fraser, __, Molly Forsyth, ?Cameron, Hector Murray, __, Janet Gammie, Anna MacLennan, __, May Matheson, Cathie Mitchell, Marion MacKenzie.
Front Row: Frankie Black, Donnie Kirk, Alec Fraser, Alick MacLeod, John Black, Pat Meldrum, Murdo Matheson, Ronnie MacKenzie, Tommy Paterson, __.

On 28th December Mr Murray recorded that the large room was very cold, the temperature being $40°F$. Christmas Day had been a holiday but the school was open on the 26th and 27th before closing again on the 28th until 8th January for New Year holidays.

When frosty weather came the children had great fun sliding on the ice on the main road – few cars then. Most of the boys wore 'tackety' boots.

Christina Nairne who was school cleaner resigned on 14th January 1929 and Miss Gilmour, Tore Park, was appointed at £14 per year. Shortly after resigning Miss Nairne married John MacLennan, Roadside. Both had been pupils in Tore School. Their children and two of their grandchildren were educated in Tore. Now their great-grandchildren are there. Over many years Mr and Mrs MacLennan fostered children from Glasgow.

On 14th January the temperature, *'with an extravagant fire'* was only $41°F$. Frost at the end of January resulted in the school twice being flooded when pipes burst.

In April the master recorded that the children's slates were dirty and the practice of spitting was again too common. It was tempting for children to spit on the slates to wipe them clean, a habit which was particularly problematic in a day when infectious diseases were prevalent. For this reason, in some areas slates had been prohibited more than ten years previously.

A pupil of the 1930s remembered that they had to take their slates home at weekends to scrub the wooden frame. Her brother used to put his in the ditch and collect it on Monday morning when it would be lovely and clean with the water running over it all weekend.

A girl from the 1940s recalled, *'I had a wet rag for wiping my slate and kept it damp by having it in a tin box.'* Another pupil of the forties commented, *'We were in trouble if we broke our slate pencils.'*

1929 - 30

When the school opened after the summer holidays (on 3rd September 1929) the teacher recorded that the buildings were clean and tidy but in a bad state of repair. Just over two weeks later on 20th September was the 'annual holiday'. This coincided with the Friday of the Northern Meeting in Inverness. Highland Games were held over three days. Each evening there was a Ball sometimes attended by royalty. In later years the games were replaced by a series of piping competitions. The field is still known as the Northern Meeting Park and events are still held there.

In October HMI Watson made a note on the buildings, accommodation and state of repair. He was accompanied by Mr MacKechnie, Secretary to the Scottish Education Department. When the children had their potato holidays workmen took the opportunity to install *'a modern heating apparatus in place of the obsolete fireplaces'.*

In the same month Mr Murray recorded that a new flush-closet system had been installed. These toilets were still in the same outside building the site of which was to the west of the new classroom installed in 2002. Hygiene was not given the prominence which it rightly has today. There were no wash basins – just a pump outside at the end of the building. Given the importance of playtime it was unlikely that the children would take time to go there to wash their hands. The school heating system did not extend beyond the school building so flush toilets in an outside building presented difficulties when the weather was frosty. That first winter they were out of action for several weeks.

At the same time as the flush toilets were installed a well was opened at the East End of the school – 20 feet (6.5m) from the building and 33 feet 3 inches (10.5m) deep with 28 feet 7 inches (9m) of water (after a dry season).

In the 1930s, when the school building underwent major extension, a classroom covered this well. Neil Macleod, whose father was Head-master between 1946 and 1956, told us that the water used to have to be pumped by hand – one pump in the school and one in the schoolhouse. A large tank was situated between the schoolhouse and the school to collect rainwater which was used to flush the outdoor toilets.

There was a hand pump located in the boys' cloakroom for drinking-water. A tin cup sat near it to be used by the children. How far health and hygiene practices have come, with today's dispensers of ice-cold bottled water and their supply of disposible plastic cups.

Below is a copy of a drawing found in the school Log Book.
It shows the position of the well covered over when the playground was improved in 1931-32.
In 1936 the well was covered by a new classroom.

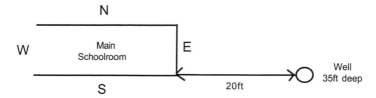

7. Uncertainty and Change

The year 1930 began badly for the school and the community and continued to be fraught with problems. On 8th January Dr Brodie carried out a medical inspection in the school and as a result one family was sent home – *'suspected infectious epidemic'*. By 31st January several cases of scarlet fever had been reported. Attendance at school was reduced and work was almost at a standstill. In those days scarlet fever was a serious illness and children infected were sent to the County Hospital in Invergordon which dealt with infectious diseases. When a child had the disease the whole family had to be kept at home to reduce the risk of it spreading. This was the case until the early 1950s. After that, although children were still sent to Invergordon and isolated, the strain seems to have been milder and less infectious. It is almost unheard of now.

On 11th March the master recorded that the attendance was,

> *worse than any we have had for over three years and this has been due in the main to the outbreaks of Scarlet Fever. Several of the children are suffering from severe colds and there is no case of absence at present due to any trivial cause and no pupils are detained at home to work.*
> *Work is very much hampered on account of the above.*

An outbreak of measles in April further reduced the attendance and when school resumed after the Easter holidays sixteen of the sixty-eight pupils were absent. In May only four pupils were presented for the 'Control' Exam. The others were prevented by measles. By the end of May only fifteen were present and on the week of 10th June that number was reduced to ten. In his summary of the school year (1929-30) the Headmaster included the fact that fifty children had suffered from measles.

On 2nd July the water supply failed. It was thought that the well had gone dry or that the pipe connecting the new system was too short in the well. The year had been very dry but the Headmaster considered that the problem was:

> *on account of w.c's, basins and hot water system in the house which creates a greater demand for the use of the bath, than when there was only a cold supply.*

Ronnie MacKenzie recalled how two of the older boys used to be sent to the schoolhouse to pump the water for the house and the school. They liked doing this. Was it a way of getting out of lessons for a while? He also remembered the well going dry and Mr Matheson, Architect, looking at a source of water in the wood at Muckernich to see whether it would be possible to supply the school from there.

There was an intriguing comment relating to an Education Authority circular about 'Intervals'. Although in 1930 this was apparently an innovation the scheme was already in operation in the school. An Inspector's visit in 1926 had led to the establishment of a ten-minute morning interval but in the ensuing years there seemed to be development of the idea. Mr Murray was of the opinion that the scheme *amply justifies itself. 11 am − 5 mins, 12 noon − 10 mins, 3 pm− 5 mins'.*

It would be interesting to know how he measured its success although we can imagine that giving the children a few minutes freedom to let off steam might pay dividends. It may also have meant less disruption from pupils asking out to the toilet during class.

Uncertainty and change

The thirties was a decade of uncertainty and of change. Nearly twelve years had passed since the end of the first World War and the world should have been recovering. However, in America, the economy was in trouble (the Great Depression) and Britain's was shaky. In Germany a man called Adolf Hitler was gathering his troops.

The *Ross-shire Journal* of 19th June 1931 reported that it cost £17 per year to educate each pupil whereas in 1918 the figure had been £3. In the 1930s wages for women teachers were relatively low − £130 per annum. From October 1931 teachers' salaries were cut. We can imagine what that did for their morale.

Motorbikes were popular and those produced at this time were either 350 or 500 cc. In 1930 the minimum age for driving a motorbike was raised from fourteen to sixteen. A frequent comment in the reminiscences of Miss MacLennan's former pupils (especially from the boys) referred to her arrival at school each day, from Evanton, on a motorbike.

A draft Highway Code was issued in 1930. That this was considered necessary, indicates the increase of motorised traffic on the roads. No Highway Code had been necessary for horse-drawn carriages and carts. In 1930 an Austin Seven cost £140 − more than the annual salary of a woman teacher. The writer's father remembers the first car in the Black Isle, possibly the first in Ross-shire. Belonging to the Fletchers of Rosehaugh it bore the registration number plate JS 1. In 1903 the first car to be registered in Inverness had been given the number ST 1. Because the licensing authorities were running out of numbers, three-letter registration plates were introduced in 1932 but it was 1939 before Inverness required to move on to AST1 and probably much later in Ross-shire before AJS 1 appeared. In 1934 compulsory driving tests were introduced. These were suspended during the war years.

This was the decade of *The Hobbit* (1937) and *Swallows and Amazons* and *The Chalet* series of books.

1930

Back Row: __, Alastair MacLennan, Adam Forsyth, Donald MacKenzie, Alec Sutherland, John MacRae, James Forsyth, Alec Paterson,__, __, __, Alfred Park, Miss MacGregor, Miss MacLennan.
2nd Row: Madda Fraser, Agnes MacKenzie, Peedie Cameron, Dolly Munro, Joey MacKenzie, Ina Fraser, Rena Macrae, Frances Cameron, Betty Gammie, Janet Park, Barbara Johnstome, Cathie Johnstone, Marion MacKenzie, Mary Murray, __.
3rd Row: Cathie Macrae, Chrissie Sutherland, __, __, Janet Gammie, __, __, May Matheson, __, Greta Johnstone, Pearl Harper, Anna MacLennan, __, __, Mina Fraser, __, Lily Fraser, Mr Murray.
Front Row: Donnie Kirk, __, Roddie MacLeod, Murdo Matheson, __, Tommy Paterson, Fraser Stewart, Dougal Cameron, Finlay MacLennan, __, __, ? Forsyth, Ronnie MacKenzie.

1930-31

After the summer holidays Miss MacLennan was transferred to Killearnan to replace a teacher who was *'off duty'*. She remained there until March 1931. The roll in Tore had been down to fifty-five which did not at that time justify three teachers. On 12th December Miss MacGregor resigned and three days later Miss Munro from Conon arrived to take her classes. Miss MacGregor was married in Newtonmore on 19th December to Allan Cameron, who belonged to the Black Isle but was a police constable in Edinburgh.

On 6th January 1931 Miss Isabella Pirie from Kyle Public School took up duties in the Infant Department, replacing Miss MacGregor. She lodged with Mrs MacLennan, Bogroy Cottage, and walked to school through the fields as did the children from Bogroy and Linnie.

On 5th January, when school resumed after the Christmas and New Year holidays, the following was entered in the Log Book.

> *Much regret was expressed at the sudden passing on 31st ult.*
> *of Dr Brodie, the respected S.M.O. for whom the children had*
> *a deep affection.*

The Executive Officer, Dr Philip, visited the school on 28th January. He complained about several of the pupils being late but Mr Murray explained that the roads were very bad, especially the cart tracks along which many of the children had to walk. *'The ground was in a slushy condition following a thaw.'* The playground resembled *'a quagmire'*. In December Mr Murray had recorded that the school was *'not in a clean and sanitary state'* because of the muddy surroundings of the school.

Miss Davidson was at the school in January and she gave a talk to the pupils about health habits. When the weather or the state of the playground was unfavourable Drill was taken in the classrooms or, as in this case, a talk was given.

After the Easter holidays (13th April) fires in the rooms were discontinued – provided the weather remained favourable. They were lit around the 15th October.

On Saturday 23rd May the school was opened to ensure that there would be the necessary four hundred openings for the year and yet be able to close at summer with the other schools in the new Avoch District. The school had been transferred from Conon District to Avoch District which had fixed the holidays for about a week earlier. Mr Gillanders who was Clerk to the Education Committee visited the school during that opening. Was he checking that it did in fact open – or how many children attended?

The school was flooded on 15th June after heavy rain because there were no drains to take away the water. This event was reported to the Education Committee – as had been done on a previous occasion when no action had been taken to improve matters.

The *Ross-shire Journal* of 26th June reported a fete and Sports held in the hotel field at Tore. This was to raise money for the Killearnan Public Hall (which was to cost £700) and for Tore United Football Club. Mr Murray, the Schoolmaster, was Secretary of the Committee for this event and many local people were involved in running *'all kinds of stalls'*.

1931 - 32

The new school year started on 25th August 1931. During the holidays the school had been painted but a ventilation problem had not been dealt with and no steps had been taken to improve the condition of the playground. The staff had hoped that this would have been attended to over the summer.

Three weeks into the school year, the nurse visited and there was reference to the improved tone of the school regarding personal appearance. Her work was given credit for this. Dr Johnston, Schools Medical Officer, carried out medical examinations on 30th September. He had been appointed in place of the late Dr Brodie and it was his first visit to the school.

In 1931 the National Mod was held in Dingwall from 22nd to 25th September so on the 25th the school was closed to allow children and parents to attend. This day was given instead of the annual holiday which would normally have been on the 18th September.

The later months of 1931 had their share of problems. As usual in October potato lifting reduced attendance. The weather was cold but because there was no firewood there could be no fires. This situation went on into November. No mention is made of whose responsibility it was to order or provide firewood.

By late November the playground was being described as a *'deplorable mess'*. Several children were wet daily through falling on the slippery mud.

It appeared, however, that improvements were imminent. By 23rd December the County Road Surveyor and staff were repairing the playground. The Architect overseeing this work was Mr Matheson. The whole surface was evened off and entirely boxed with stone carted *(by horse-drawn cart)* from Kilcoy Quarry or brought by motor lorry from Tarradale Quarry.

The following February the 'boxing' was overlaid with a coat of small rubble from the quarry beyond Rosemarkie and it was recorded, *'to date about three hundred tons of material has been brought.'* In mid-April the surface was dressed with crusher dust. The day after this was done, the Chairman of the Property and Works committee of the County Council visited with the Architect to examine the work. The Headmaster was advised to keep the children off the playground until the dust settled but as he pointed out that was not practical and the surveyor who supervised the work had advocated as much tramping as possible.

December had brought other problems. While the playground was being improved the boiler for the heating system blew up. This meant that for three days they were unable to have a fire in the larger room. In the morning the older pupils joined the younger ones in the smaller room and *'suitable instruction was given in accordance with the overcrowded conditions and mixed classes'*. In the afternoon the children met in Killearnan Hall for oral work and singing. There they had the advantage of the piano.

This new hall had been opened two weeks earlier on Saturday 5th December by Mrs Fraser-Mackenzie of Allangrange. The opening was followed by a sale of work 'and other attractions'. The following week a Grand Concert and Dance was held in the hall.

The children's Christmas treat was, for the first time, held in the hall and the tree was supplied by the Fraser-MacKenzies, from a wood on the Allangrange Estate.

Alister MacKenzie, Muckernich, was one of the younger children at the time. He has memories of playing on the foundations when the hall was being built.

Over the Christmas holidays a new boiler was installed. The previous one had come, second-hand, from Cromarty School. A rubber washer had caused the stoppage and this had led to destruction of the boiler.

On 5th February, 1932, the teacher noted that the East wind made its first appearance of the year. There was a marked fall in attendance following the spell of Easterly winds which brought colds and other illnesses.

At 12.30 pm on Thursday 19th May a mysterious situation occurred. The Headmaster discovered that Miss Pirie's class had been left with no teacher in charge. She had not given notice that she was going out of school nor did the Headmaster know of any reason why she should go. We can imagine his consternation at this state of affairs but he must have also been rather concerned for his assistant. The following day Miss Pirie reported for duty as usual but an explanation was required. She had gone to a funeral. She seems to have been forgiven for her oversight in not informing her superior.

1932-33

After the summer holidays of 1932 the nine pupils in the Advanced Division (post-qualifying class) were sent by bus to Munlochy School because of congestion in Tore. Four Glasgow boarded-out children from Linnie were sent to Killearnan School. There were then seventy-two children on the roll.

On 21st September the school was closed in the afternoon in recognition of the centenary of the death of the Scottish writer, Sir Walter Scott. It is possible that his novels were part of the library which had over a number of years disappeared to nothing. *Ivanhoe* and *Rob Roy* were well known to children of the time and his poem, *The Lady of the Lake,* was included in the curriculum for older pupils.

The perennial problem arose of absence for potato-lifting and the entry added: *'Children from 5 to 12 years old are being employed at potato lifting.'*

In December concern was again expressed about the ventilation in the larger room. Because of that and the overcrowding the children were being given an extended interval *'in open air'*.

When the school opened on 10th January 1933, having been closed from 23rd December, Mr Murray recorded that the teachers had benefited from the longer holiday and the children looked well. The weather had been fine and open which would have contributed to this.

In January there was a visit from Mr Matheson, Architect, to measure the height of the ceiling and windows in the large room with a view to improving the ventilation. A year was to pass before a new ventilator was fitted and it did not solve the problem. The light also was unsatisfactory.

An Inspector's visit on 20th January left the staff with the feeling that the better children had not done themselves justice while the poorer ones had done better than expected. The teachers knew their pupils and believed that they were more able to assess them. In spite of their fears, the report on the progress of the different classes received in March was positive.

> *An attempt has been made to relieve the congestion in this*
> *school by sending post-qualifying pupils elsewhere. Since then,*
> *however, there have been many further enrolments, and the*
> *numbers now are much as they were before with the result*

that the accommodation is again strained. The question should engage the Education Authority's attention, as soon as conditions allow. In the senior room the desks are antiquated and the seats without backs. It is urgently necessary that at least two forms with back supports should be provided at once, to keep the children in the rear seats from touching the hot water pipes, and new desks should be provided for all the pupils as soon as practicable. The arrangement of the seats in this room is bad, as the children sit facing south with the sun straight in their eyes.

In the lowest section, pleasing results have been achieved in all the main subjects.

The work of the middle and senior sections is rendered difficult by the presence of two teachers in one room which is of only moderate size. In spite of this, a decided improvement has taken place in the work of the middle section since the date of the last report, and both arithmetic and spelling are accurate. In the two top senior classes, arithmetic and spelling are also satisfactory.... Grammar might be further advanced at this stage. Composition exercises show sound teaching method.

Photograph: Scholastic Souvenir Co.

Back Row: Donald Mackenzie, Alec Fraser, Alister Henderson, Dougal Cameron, Murdo Matheson, Alec MacLeod, Tommy Paterson, Donnie Kirk, Ronnie MacKenzie, Arthur Park, John Kirk, Andrew Matheson.

2nd Row: Marjory MacGregor, Marion MacKenzie, Janet Gammie, Molly Forsyth, Chrissie Sutherland, Chrissie MacCulloch, Ina Penman, Violet Hardie, Lily Fraser, Ellen Black, Miss MacLennan.

3rd Row: __, __, Margaret Forsyth, Lizzie Meldrum, May MacKenzie, __, Greta Johnstone, ?Cuthbertson, Cathie Mitchell, Nan McCombie, Mina Fraser, Anna Kirk, Mary Murray, Jean Dalgetty, Miss Pirie, Jessie Dalgetty.

4th Row: Andrew Gammie, Archie Bruce, __ , Pat Kirk, Hector Murray, Henry McCombie, John Hardie, D.D. Forsyth, Pat Meldrum, Johnnie Dalgetty, Bobby Black.

Front Row: Mr Murray, __, Christobel Murray, Alistair Bruce, Bertie Henderson, Gordy Forsyth, Billy?, Bobby Russell, Alister MacKenzie, Robert Hardie, John Ross, Jimmy Henderson, Bob Halliday.

Football Team 1933

Back Row;
Pat Meldrum,
Alister Henderson,
Donnie Kirk,
Dougal Cameron,
Murdo Matheson,
Alec MacLeod

Front Row;
Bobby Black,
Alec Fraser,
D.D. Forsyth,
John Hardie,
Ronnie MacKenzie

Towards the end of February the boiler again blew off a quantity of water. Frost was blamed. It happened on Wednesday 22nd, the day in which school was closing for the sacraments weekend. The Headmaster considered this *'fortunate from the standpoint of openings'*. The regulation of four hundred half-day openings seems to have been rigidly observed.

On 18th April fires were discontinued although the weather was still cold. The coal was *'dross and dust unfit for burning'*. The inside temperature was recorded as 53° which was lower than some of the winter temperatures.

Some of the boys discarded their boots at the end of April and were barefooted throughout the four summer months. The soles of their feet were like leather.

The weather improved as the year progressed and in June because of the dryness of the season the well ran dry. On the 30th of that month Mr Murray desribed the weather conditions as perfect. When the children returned to school in August during exceptionally fine weather he noted that they looked well.

1933 - 34   How nice the big girls were to me

One of the 1933 infants, Jean Dalgetty, now Mrs Cameron, has never forgotten how nice the older girls were to her when she went to school. Her older sister, Jessie, was already attending the school. The 'big girls' were always very good about looking after the new intake.

On 12th September the water supply again gave out during *'exceedingly dry and hot weather but by careful supervision of the use of lavatories and disuse of wash hand basins the amount collected overnight suffices for necessary purposes'*.

The Headteacher noted that Primary 1 was *'much too large for this school.'* The solution was to split it in two, the better half to proceed with normal work, the rest to join them as they proved fit. Primary 1 was then the first class in the Junior Section, after the two infant classes.

By mid-September he was aware that the Junior Section was *'much above the average in natural ability as far as this school area is concerned and is by far the best group of pupils this school has had for several years'.*

In late September the potato-lifting at Croftcrunie and Tore Mains affected attendance and in November Mr Murray noted, concerning attendance, *'Constant supervision is absolutely necessary if a favourable record is to be maintained.'*

On Wednesday 18th October the Lower and Middle sections received an extra half-hour singing – from 2.30 to 3 pm. Then on 20th December it was recorded that:

> *Extra periods are devoted to singing and dramatic work at present for Christmas Concert given by the children, which is a profitable way of getting the most out of a short day during which it is not possible to continue ordinary written work in a room where the lighting is anything but perfect.*

Jean Cameron remembers taking part in a school performance. She wore a pink dress and stood on a chair to sing. Archie Bruce has a clear memory of Tommy Paterson as a sweep (all black) and Johnnie Hardie as a meal miller (all white) making a dramatic collision on the middle of the stage. Their performance merited a big cheer from the audience. His own little brother, Sinclair, very small with blond hair was lifted on to the stage by Miss Pirie. He wore a little red suit and began by saying, *'I'm such a little tot, I don't know if you see me or not.'* Nan MacCombie also sang. Murdo Ross, who worked on Allangrange Estate, was Santa. He had a beard so all he needed was a red cloak and hood. He always wore plus-fours but one little chap went home and told his parents he wore 'class fives'. That same little chap (Archie Bruce) was to sell many pairs of plus-fours in his trade.

Murdo Ross's daughter is remembered in the Beatrice Percival Memorial Prize at Aberdeen University. This prize was established by her son, Ian, a top geologist with Shell and a former pupil of Tore School.

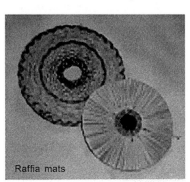

Raffia mats

On 26th January 1934 the Executive Officer called with samples of handwork – wool, raffia and paper – and expressed the desire to see this implemented in the infant room. The middle section was already involved but the upper section did no handwork. The Headmaster acknowledged that it could be undertaken if there was a suitable accommodation area. About two weeks later handwork was introduced in the infant room. Some people still have in their possession raffia mats made at this time.

June of that year was very warm and the master was concerned about pupils being confined in the inadequate space for any length of time. There were sixty-four children on the roll.

1934 - 35

At the end of 1934 the winter was severe, with a snowstorm on 1st November. The midday interval was scrapped and pupils were dismissed at 2 o'clock. Jean Cameron tells of her mother putting stockings over her boots to cover the tops to stop the snow going in.

The following comment came from Archie Bruce.

> *Armistice Day was strictly observed on 11th November at 11am Mr Murray rang a handbell and we all stood for one minute's silence. I can remember being quite moved on such an occasion.*

On 20th November the Headteacher wrote that there were forty-three pupils in the upper room and two teachers.

> *This room would not adequately accommodate under modern conditions any more than thirty pupils and even the light is bad, heating very unsatisfactory and ventilation primitive.*

The children were given a holiday on 29th November for the wedding of the King's youngest son, HRH Duke of Kent and Princess Marina of Greece.

In December the boiler was again destroyed due to a defect. Because of lack of heating the school was too cold for the children so the Christmas holidays began a day early on 20th December. The boiler was replaced by a new one in January but, according to the Headmaster, no attempt was made to rectify the defective system to prevent a repeat of the problems.

In 1935 'Cats'-eyes' were first used to mark the middle of the road – another indicator of the increasing number of motor vehicles on the roads.

Robert Watson-Watt developed radar, whereby he could detect planes at a distance of seventy miles, a system which was going to help Britain and her allies win a future war.

When she visited the school in March Miss Davidson suggested buying more equipment for Drill, such as ropes and balls, but the Headmaster thought there was ample equipment. He also believed that equipment for school use should be provided by the Education Committee.

In April a note in the Log Book recorded,

> *In the middle section of the school discipline, although the word savours of an age that has passed, has had to be tightened up and is receiving the attention of the Headmaster.*

Earlier in the session, in November, he had written, *'The Headmaster was almost wholly occupied in discipline matters.'*

There is no truth in the belief that children in the past were all well-behaved in school, deterred by the threat of the tawse.

The weather at this time was cold and snow was falling. There was illness – chest and throat infections.

The children appear to take ill without much indication of trouble and several are absent.

Because of this, in consultation with the Executive Officer, it was decided that the school should close for Easter on 5th instead of 18th April. Can we imagine the uproar today if that was suggested? Parents and children have holidays planned; childminders are lined up; teachers have holidays booked. End-of-term events would have to be postponed. It could not happen.

It was common for Infants to be sent to school in the course of the summer term. Some enrolled after the Easter break but others arrived well into the term. A girl of the 1930s wrote the following verse.

I went to school to do my a b c
I cried, I laughed, I giggled
I bumped my head, I cried again
and that was me.
<u>Christobel Murray</u>

Infant's chair, with prize book and Bible

Monday 6th May was the King's Silver Jubilee. All the children in the Parish – about two hundred in all – from Tore, Killearnan and Arpafeelie Schools, some from Munlochy School and the pre-school children along with adults gathered at Redcastle grounds.

The day was ideal and the setting perfect.

Sports were held for children and adults, tea and good things to eat were provided, and each child received a *'handsome china souvenir mug and Jubilee medal'.* Mr Murray described the whole event as, *'A day in school history.'*

That evening a huge bonfire was lit on Gallowhill. One local man who worked on Redcastle Estate recalled his stint the previous night guarding the bonfire in case someone tried to set it alight. His companion, an older estate worker, had taken along a bottle of rum with which they fortified themselves through the long hours.

Ten days later the weather had turned bitterly cold and there were heavy snowstorms on the hills. The lowest temperature for the season for sixty-four years was recorded at Kew. The fires were restarted but by 6 pm room temperature had failed to reach 62° F.

1935 - 36

Classes resumed on 28th August after the holidays during which there had been an epidemic of whooping cough.

On 12th September Mr Matheson, Architect, and an assistant visited the school in connection with the proposed renovations. Overcrowding had long been a problem, resulting in the transfer of pupils, but at last some action was being taken.

The school was closed on Friday 20th September. *The Friday of the Northern Meeting is observed as the annual holiday here.'*

A week later the weather was cold so fires were lit. Mr Murray recorded that the weather had been broken since August 27th and most of the harvest was still in the stook. This happened frequently and even in October farmers might be struggling, because of poor weather, to take in their corn.

In October HMI Grieve visited. He disapproved of pupils being absent for the potato harvest but the matter was already before the Council although Headmasters had not been made aware of the decision. On 31st December a communication arrived from the Executive Officer concerning the Authority's byelaws on the employment of young people. One relevant clause stated that children under twelve could only be employed by parents or Guardians.

1935/36

Photograph: Scholastic Souvenir Co.

Back Row: Robert Hardie, Johnnie Dalgetty, Archie Bruce, Andrew Matheson, John Ross, Andrew Gannie, Hector Murray, Bertie Henderson, Miss Pirie.
2nd Row: Henry MacCombie, Pat Dalgetty, Sandy Sutherland, Willie Halliday, Jean Dalgetty, Jem MacEwen, Jetta Forsyth, Billy MacEwen, James MacCulloch, Sinclair Bruce, Peter Maclean, Ian MacLennan
Front Row: Gordon Forsyth, Margaret Hardie, Christobel Murray, Alistair Bruce.

In November a School Population Table (Page 199) was drawn up. Children were classed as floating or permanent. The 'floating' population were those who had come from other schools. Those designated 'permanent' had never been to any other school. Altogether there were forty permanent pupils and twenty-six floating. As we have considered the frequency with which farm workers changed their employer it is not surprising that nearly half the school population had already been at other schools.

The Population Table also showed that out of a total of sixty-six children nineteen were in Class V. This was due to some children beyond the age of twelve remaining in Tore School.

History in the making

On Sunday 19th January 1936 the weather turned stormy and because of snow the school closed early on Monday. The following day there was a severe blizzard and snowdrifts blocked the roads. Several pupils were unable to attend school. That day the Headmaster recorded,

> *It is with profound regret that the news of the death of His Majesty King George V which took place early this morning at Sandringham is received by the staff and pupils of this school. The children called him a 'good King'.*

He was succeeded by his eldest son who became King Edward VIII.

On 28th January the school closed for the King's funeral. Mr Murray refers to him as, '*His late Majesty of proud memory.*'

The new King created a constitutional crisis. He was in love with an American divorcee, Mrs Simpson, whom he wanted to marry. Because it was not permissible for a member of the British Royal Family to marry a divorcee he decided to give up the throne rather than live without her. In December, after eleven months as King, he abdicated and his brother, the Duke of York, became King George VI.

Building Reconstruction

Dr Philip, Executive Officer, called at the school on 18th March 1936 and inspected the Public Hall with a view to using it when the school building was being reconstructed. On May 11th the hall was taken over for school purposes and since there were three teachers it was divided by curtains to separate the groups. One boy of the time clearly remembers these *big green curtains*. Others have made comments which indicate how ineffective these were as partitions. They could hear what was going on in the other areas; older pupils bumped the younger ones through the curtains and pupils were even known to have fallen off their forms and into the next section.

In August 1936 classes resumed after the summer holidays with seventy-five children on the roll. Two days after the start of the session the temperature inside the hall, with all doors and windows fully open, was 84°F at 12 o'clock. The children were allowed to remain outside for extended periods. By 2 pm the temperature had reached 86°F.

A month later the weather was cold and the central heating in the hall was on. Lessons continued there until November. The following comment was received from a pupil of that time:

> *The building of the 'new' school was exciting. I used to admire the skill of the bricklayers. Jock the Quarry had the contract.*

On 27th November the school building was ready to re-open and the children were sent home early so that the contractors could remove the school furniture from the Hall and return it to the school. On 30th November the Headmaster wrote:

> *The reconstructed school was opened today after extensive alterations etc. which have been going on since 11th May last. A new classroom has been added to the East end, the front wall entirely removed to foundation and a new front built into the old school which now forms the middle and west rooms.*
> *The old school has been divided evenly into two rooms in place of the former large or East room and small or West room. Cross-draught windows are added and the whole back structure, also the three east lavatories.*
> *There was evidence in the old walls of at least two previous reconstructions and the whitewash on bare stone walls and clay floor shows that the building is very old. The present floor has been raised some ten inches above the level of the last which in turn was about the same height above the old clay floor.*
> *Contractors: Mason John Fraser, Kilcoy; Carpenter Macrae and Sons, Beauly; Slater Simon Fraser, Dingwall; Plasterer Reid, Alness; Painter Tom MacDonald, Avoch; Asphalt Briggs, Dundee; Heating R. Mackenzie and Sons, Dingwall.*

The back structure which had been added included the corridor, cloakrooms for boys and girls and the staff room. The additional lavatories must have been for the boys since the girls' lavatories were situated on the west side. They were still not attached to the school building.

The reference to whitewash on walls reminds us that in 1884 an Inspector in his report recommended that the walls be whitewashed and the children

New Building 1936
Mrs Murray and Miss Pirie

discouraged from writing on them. There had been an extended summer holiday that year while repairs to the school were carried out. The reference to two previous reconstructions is intriguing. In Chapter 5 there was reference to one major change around 1910.

The earliest work may have been the building of a slate roof to replace the thatched one as required by the title deeds (1882).

The Headmaster complained in January 1937 that workmen who were putting a new body on the pump and working on the heating system were disfiguring the new walls. This was discouraging when teachers and pupils were making an effort to *'maintain the beauty of the amenities'*.

Ink

On 11th March 1937, *'Writing in ink having attention in Class II and III'*, was the first reference to the use of ink. There were holes in the desks for inkwells (made of metal or china). The pens had wooden handles and nibs. Fountain pens, although invented in 1884, were not common at this time and even in the fifties pupils had to learn to write with plain pens. By the time they sat the Qualifying Examination they were allowed to use fountain pens. Although ballpoint pens, invented by Biro, had appeared in the 1930s pupils were **not** allowed to use these for any ink work in school. The nibs of the old-fashioned pens sometimes scratched the paper, or spattered inkblots on work that was expected to be pristine. It was heartbreaking to see painstaking work marred by the use of a less than perfect nib. The inkwells were a problem too. Bits of rubber found their way in and gunge settled on the bottom. Ink sometimes came in powdered form and was made up by adding water. It tended to dry out and leave sediment.

> *I remember on one occasion the inkwell in my desk was jammed and I played with it trying to get it loose. It suddenly dislodged*

and flew into the air in an arc leaving a residue of ink as it went. I can still see the Headmaster charging up the aisle between the desks and demanding to know if I was trying to do conjuring tricks.

In December 1937 there was such a severe frost that the ink stocks froze and caused damage to adjacent stock.

Problems

Dr Johnston School Medical Officer called on 16th March and noted a number of things: lack of water *'for closets and other purposes'*, and the effects of the heating furnace on the health of pupils. Several pupils were suffering headaches and some from stomach trouble. This must have been a very disappointing situation in light of the recent improvements to the school building. Dr Johnston instructed the Headmaster to let the pupils out if ill effects were noted and he would inform the Architect about the problems. The furnace was situated in the new room which had been added at the East of the school. Since there were three teachers at this time the older pupils were being taught in this room.

Two days after Dr Johnston's visit the Chairman of the Education Committee, Rev Dr Dow, called and discussed with the Headmaster the heating, lighting, ventilation and water supply of the new school. The well was now under the new building.

Dr Dow was minister of the old church near Bogallan from 1892 until 1938 when, at the age of seventy-five, he died. The manse where he lived is still there as are the ruins of the Church.

Coronation

The school had a holiday in May (12th to 14th) 1937 for the Coronation (on the 12th) of King George and his Queen, Elizabeth. Attending that Coronation, as an eleven-year-old, was their daughter, Princess Elizabeth, heir to the throne (and now Queen herself). There was a celebration, with sports, at Redcastle for the children of the Parish.

In July of that year the use of the number 999 for emergency calls went into operation.

Children at Tore Hall - waiting for transport to Redcastle

Potato holidays seem to have been in abeyance at this time but exemption was given for older children. On 6th October the school was closed because of an outbreak of scarlet fever and did not open again until the 18th.

On 1st November Miss Marshall, needlework inspectress, visited the school. The girls were taught by one of the female teachers, Miss Pirie or Miss MacLennan, while the boys did handwork – in raffia or cane. There are still in existence some of the items made by boys, as this small tray.

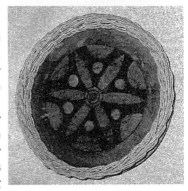

The girls first sewed lapbags to hold their future sewing and knitting. They made aprons in Standard 5, in preparation for cookery in the later classes. The older girls made nightdresses and underwear. Knitting usually began with a simple scarf and as the girls progressed they made mitts and socks.

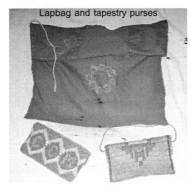

Lapbag and tapestry purses

Two days, 4th and 5th November, were given as holidays for harvest thanksgiving. A week later the Headmaster recorded that the temperature for the week had been so low (40°- 48°F) that work did not go on as usual. On 30th November the attendance was the lowest of his eleven years in the school. This was because of an epidemic and there were '*certified cases of chill*".

The *Wizard* and the *Hotspur* were boys' comics of the thirties but in December 1937 a new comic for children was published by D.C. Thomson in Dundee. It was called the *Dandy* and was such a success that it was followed in July 1938 by the *Beano*.

A story is told of an assistant teacher who was left in charge on a Friday afternoon while the Headteacher attended a meeting. The class had been provided with work and the assistant teacher was to look in on them occasionally. In the course of the afternoon a man whom she did not recognise came through the school gate and as he approached the building she went into the corridor to meet him. Her heart sank when she realised he was an Inspector. Her thoughts flashed to those children in the Headmaster's room who might be doing their work but, on the other hand, might be reading the comics which they bought on Fridays. To her relief she found that they were all busy working on the assigned tasks. Were the children a step ahead? Had they seen the man and suspected he was an Inspector?

On 23rd December, *'Severe frost held the district in its grip for the past three weeks and owing to the poor heating of the school, classes were dismissed before 2 o'clock.'* The temperature was down to 31°F. This was the time when the ink froze.

School closed for the Christmas and New Year holidays *'after the children were entertained to tea and the usual fare of the season'.*

Miss MacLennan, as a member of Voluntary Aid Department, Red Cross, was given leave of absence to attend the Empire Exhibition held from 7th to 10th June 1938 in Glasgow.

1938 - 39

The summer of 1938 was wet and lacking in sunshine yet when the school reopened on 23rd August the children looked well and fit. The weather improved and on 8th September the teacher noted that there was bright sunshine with a clear sky and only one pupil was absent. Early October was, however, cold and wet and in the first week the fires were already on. On 1st November the Headmaster reported wild showers of sleet and hail. *'Much corn is still uncut and more in stook.'*

Miss Pirie was transferred to Killen School from Monday 10th October because there had been a drop in the roll at Tore (down to fifty-two).

The school closed from 2nd to 8th November for the mid-term break which coincided with the Harvest Thanksgiving holiday. On the 2nd Miss MacLennan who had been on the staff *'since Nov 3rd 1926 (exactly 12 years to a day) with the exception of a break ... left to take up duties in Conon P. School.'* Miss MacLennan lived to the age of ninety-four. She died in 1997.

A story is told by one of her pupils. Miss MacLennan asked her class, 'Who fought at the battle of Culloden?'

One little girl whispered something to her pal who immediately shot up her hand and was asked for her answer.

'Benny Lynch and Small Montana.'

Those two flyweight boxers had earlier competed for the world championship. (Benny Lynch, from Glasgow, had won.)

Miss Pirie returned from Killen on 8th November to take over Miss MacLennan's duties. One of her pupils recalled that she drove a Singer car.

If 1938 had been fairly uneventful, 1939 more than compensated.

The school was due to open on 10th January but there had been a severe snowstorm. The Headmaster was away from home and was snowed up. On his return he discovered that thirteen of the eighteen radiators had been destroyed by frost and the pump supplying the system was also damaged and out of order. The fire had gone out owing to lack of draught while the thermometer registered 22°F, ten degrees below freezing. The heating system was not repaired until January 19th.

On 28th January Miss Pirie was absent and she remained absent for nearly three months. The Headmaster was teaching the whole school himself although no room was considered large enough. Help arrived on the afternoon of 6th March in the person of Miss A. C. MacLeod from North Tolsta Primary School, Lewis. Schools on the Island of Lewis at that time were the responsibility of Ross and Cromarty Education Authority. It was only in 1975, under regionalisation, that they were transferred to a new Western Isles Council. A month after taking up duties in Tore Miss MacLeod transferred to Invergordon Academy. Miss H. Young, MA, Fortrose, taught the younger classes until Miss Pirie resumed work on 21st April.

All these changes in staff were likely to have a detrimental effect on progress and at the end of March the record in the Log Book referred to this and to the poor attendance of the children due to an epidemic.

On 19th May the local Mod was held in Dingwall. The school was closed that day since the pupils wished to have their holiday then instead of the annual local holiday normally held on the 15th. In 1911 there had been a reference to the holiday for Empire Day on 26th May. That annual holiday around 15th may have been a continuation of that tradition.

On 2nd June the Headmaster recorded that the temperature inside the rooms that week was up to 74° F with all doors and windows fully open. Outside in the sun the temperature reading was 94°F. The teacher recorded that the work was modified to suit although he did not specify how the work was carried out.

School trips were not frequent but one former pupil recalled a day at Rosemarkie. They walked from the school to Allangrange Station and travelled by train to Fortrose. From there they walked to Rosemarkie where they had a picnic on the beach.

Below are two photos from the 1930s. Unfortunately the first is only a photocopy since the original could not be tracked down.

1938/39

Back Row: Annie Henderson, Dolly Sutherland, Sybil Henderson, Margaret Hardie, Jean MacKenzie, Bella Macphee, __, Kate Macphee (at back), Betty Reid, __, Bertha Murray, __, Helen Borland, __, __.
Front Row: __, __, Jimmy Rennie, Willie Ian Dalgetty, Sandy Sutherland, __, George Borland, Roy MacRae, Sinclair Bruce, Eck MacPhee, __, __.

1938/39

Back Row: Mary Meldrum, Ellen Miller, ? Stark, ? Stark, Chrissie MacCulloch, Bunty Rugg, Jean Dalgetty, Agnes Rennie, Christobel Murray.
Middle Row: Tommy Miller,Hector Murray, Sandy Macrae, Archie Bruce, Jimmy Henderson, Richard Miller, Robert Hardie, John Dalgetty, Bert Henderson, Duncan ?, Pat Dalgetty.
Front Row: Hughie MacDonald, Alistair Bruce, Sinclair Bruce.

Examples of early basket work
crafted by boys while girls
were taught needlework

From a photograph by N.U.T.

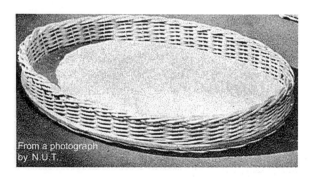

From a photograph by N.U.T.

97

8. The War Years

A year to forget 1939 - 40

The early months of 1939 were times of uncertainty for the country because of events in Europe. The school reopened, after the summer holidays, on Tuesday 29th August. War was declared on Sunday 3rd September.

> *Owing to the outbreak of war between this country and Germany this school in common with others was closed for the week ending Friday September 8th.*

On Tuesday 12th September the school Log Book entry read: *'The Headmaster is called up from HM reserve of Officers for active service to report to Headquarters, Golspie, today.'*

This is rather a poignant entry because Mr Murray did not return from the war.

When he left on the 12th Miss Pirie took charge as Headteacher and for a week she taught all the classes herself until Miss Reid joined her as teacher of the older children. Miss Reid lived in Dingwall with her sister who taught piano.

On 29th September they tried out the heating system in preparation for the winter and discovered it was not in good working order. Dr Thomson, Director of Education, called at the school and he noted the unsatisfactory state of the water supply. Two weeks later a plumber arrived and found a leak in one of the underground water pipes. The trouble continued and about a month later he mended another leak in the same pipe. He also slackened a rusty damper in the furnace and extracted from the lower part of the chimney, four or five loose pieces of slate and some lumps of lime. This rubble must have lodged there during the renovations three years before.

That, unfortunately, wasn't the end of the matter. Shortly afterwards the cleaner had trouble lighting the fire in the morning, a situation which went on for about a week. Since a dirty chimney seemed to be the cause, the sweep was sent for and finally a week later the heating system was working.

By mid December the fire had to be left on all night and required attendance late in the evening. This would, under normal circumstances, be done by a Headteacher living in the Schoolhouse but Miss Pirie lived away from the school, in lodgings at Bogroy. Alick Macrae, Tore Park, who was already responsible for pumping the water, was engaged to bank up the fire at 9.30 in the evening.

A rectangular wooden panel closing off the chimney, in the west wall of the General Purposes room, is the only evidence of the position of the furnace. This room, for many years, housed the school library. When the school roll decreased and it was no longer required as a classroom it was used for Drill on days when the weather restricted outdoor activity. (In 1956, when school dinners were started in Tore, it went into use as the dining-room and for a time in the 1960s when the school roll increased it was again put into operation as a classroom.)

Miss Paterson, the teacher of Drill, took classes at the school once every two months and between her visits the class teachers took the lessons. In October of 1939 she advised the use of more apparatus and requested large balls, wooden hoops, and beanbags. Her predecessor had not been granted these when she requested them in 1935 but since this equipment was very much part of the Drill lessons in the forties (and fifties) Miss Pirie must have acquiesced.

Miss Reid taught the children country-dances for half an hour each week and in December when Miss Paterson made her regular visit to the school she was impressed with the pupils' performance.

The local district nurse was a regular visitor to the school checking hair and fingernails and in November 1939 an entry informed, 'Nurse Weir talked to the children on laws of health.'

Rationing

Because of the War, on January 8th 1940 certain food items and clothing had to be rationed. The school became a distribution point for the books of coupons which everyone received. On one occasion the teacher noted that

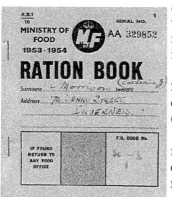

at the beginning of November Mr MacGregor, the food officer, had called and left four hundred ration books for Tore and District. Everyone, including babies, had a book.

An adult's ration of butter for the week was 2 oz (50-60 gm) and meat was 1 lb (450 gm) and cost about 1s (5p). The bacon ration was 4 oz (just under 120 gm).

The *Ross-shire Journal* ran advertisements notifying people of the arrangements for obtaining new books. For some products rationing continued until the 1950s.

Mrs Morrison, owner of this ration book, was Catherine MacKinnon, a daughter of Donald MacKinnon, the carpenter, who lived in Tore Village. Catherine attended Tore School from 1912. She finished her schooling in Killearnan school.

A fall of snow on 19th January reduced attendance, especially in the infant class, and the following week there were cases of German measles.

Because of an epidemic of measles and of influenza only one third of the pupils were present on 19th February. The Headteacher, acting on instructions from Dr Thomson, dismissed the school and reopened on Tuesday 27th although there were children still suffering from these illnesses. It happened to be the Communion weekend from 22nd to 26th February so the school would have been closed anyway, probably from Wednesday evening until Tuesday. By 4th March only one pupil was absent.

Medal Mystery

During the week ending 12th April Class V were given tests in preparation for the Qualifying Examination. One of those in Class V was Jean Dalgetty (now Mrs Cameron, Allanglach). In 1999 she wrote the following article for a Tore School Newspaper, *Talking Tore*.

"I was in my final year in Tore School in 1940 when I was twelve years old and I won the Dux medal. It was an exciting time for me, because I was moving to a new school, and travelling to and from there on a bus. This is quite usual these days, but I had always walked to school, as did everyone else, so travelling by bus every day was a big adventure.

There were momentous things happening in other parts of the world at that time, particularly in Europe, so altogether it was an exciting time to be growing up.

I got married in 1949 and moved in to the house that I'm living in now leaving my Dux medal in my parents' home, with other personal things, intending to pick them up some time later.

My mother died in 1954, and sometime after that my medal disappeared from my parents' house. I had a family of two girls and two boys, and was very busy, occasionally wondering what had happened to my medal.

During February 1998, Elizabeth Dickson, Tower Street, Golspie, found a medal on Back Road, Golspie and handed it in to the police station.

After six months no one claimed it so they gave it back to her. Elizabeth then sent a letter to the 'Ross Shire Journal', stating all the facts.

I got in touch with her then finally after fifty-eight years, I've got my Dux medal back with me.

Someone had been using it, maybe as a keyring, because it was well worn — not sparkling and shiny like the last time I saw it.

Now, of course, it is a much more interesting medal because it has a story attached to it. Who had it and how on earth did it get to Golspie?

Way more mysterious and exciting than lying in a drawer all these years.

I will never know the true story about what my Dux medal got up to, but it is nice to have it back.

There was evidence that the nation was at war. Newspapers carried big advertisements warning children to carry their gasmasks at all times.

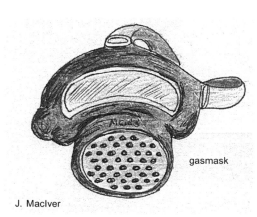

gasmask

J. MacIver

Mr McCombie, the farmer at Tore Mains, was the local County Councillor and acted as air-raid warden for the district. He called at the school at the end of May 1940 to exchange the gasmasks of several children for whom they had become too small.

Towards the end of June, on the instructions of Dr Thomson, all the school windows were pasted with brown paper as a protection against bomb splinters. John Ross, a former pupil who was then a young apprentice, recalls going to schools and putting netting on the windows for the same purpose.

June 1940 was an important time in the early days of the war when thousands of soldiers were evacuated from Dunkirk. One pupil remembers Miss Pirie closing the school early at lunchtime and hurrying home, presumably to hear the news at one o'clock.

In school there was hundred percent attendance and the area was enjoying fine weather. On June 3rd, after the May 'Term', five new children were enrolled taking the number of pupils up to forty-four.

Towards the end of the month Miss Pirie reported that, *'three children belonging to the nomad class left school.'* Some of the reasons given by earlier teachers for those children leaving were 'Summer Cruise' or 'Summer Trek'. There were several places around Tore where travelling people set up camps. As time went on they acquired caravans and were later given tenancy of Council Houses. Jean Cameron tells us that she was pally with a girl whose family lived in a tent at Kilcoy and one dinnertime instead of going home she went with her friend. She described how they sat on the bed and ate porridge which the girl's mother had prepared on a stove which stood in the middle of the floor.

A School Management Committee meeting on 22nd June decided that the school, which was closing for the summer on 4th July, should reopen on 13th August, two weeks earlier than usual. The other two weeks were to be given in the autumn. Children would then be available for helping with the harvest and potato lifting. In 1940 the remaining two weeks of the *'summer vacation'* were taken from 23rd September.

More staff changes
1940-41

Before the summer holidays Miss Pirie resigned and in July she married William MacRae, who was an engineering clerk in Glasgow but whose father was stationmaster in Kyle. Miss Pirie herself belonged to Inverness and it

was there she died in 1982 at the age of 77. Her replacement in Tore was Miss Donella Gillies, MA, BSc, who took up duty in August. She had been born in Harris in 1911 and was a graduate of Glasgow University. Miss Gillies who lived in Conon with her sister was a very small lady.

Three children from Arpafeelie and one from Conon were admitted to school a week after it opened.

On 18th October Miss Gilmour resigned as school cleaner and the following Tuesday Mr Graham, Clerk to the School Management Committee, called. Mrs Murray, the Schoolhouse, was *'very kindly'* seeing to the work. About a month later, because there was difficulty finding a suitable person, she agreed to fill the post. She had already, on 20th August, taken charge of the heating and was also pumping the water for the school.

Donella Gillies

The *Ross-shire Journal* on 3rd January 1941 reported a speech by Roosevelt, President of the United States of America, in which he uttered the prophetic words: *'I believe that the axis powers are not going to win the war.'* (The axis powers were Germany and her allies.) America entered the war in that year.

Because this was a farming area, where most of the men were employed in agricultural work, not many local men were called up for active service but became part of the Home Guard. Most of those who were conscripted – they were between eighteen and forty-one – joined the Seaforth Highlanders, the Ross-shire based regiment, although some signed up for the RAF. Throughout the war the *Ross-shire Journal* carried lists of men from the county, mainly from the Seaforths – missing, killed, wounded, or taken prisoner-of-war. Some former pupils of the school spent time in prisoner-of-war camps. Archie Kirk and Evan MacRae were taken prisoner at St Valery. Archie spent the remainder of the war in a POW camp in Poland. The *Ross-shire* also carried a table showing blackout times.

One interesting coincidence from the war was the meeting in North Africa of two men who had spent some time as pupils in the school, George MacKenzie (son of Dolly Paterson featured in chapter 3) and Finlay MacLennan. What made the encounter more amazing was that Finlay's home was then in South Africa and he was serving as a navigator with the South African Air Force. After the War George lived for many years in Australia.

Local news reported in February included problems with the Kessock Ferry boat which was an important link for North Kessock and the Black Isle with Inverness, particularly when few people had cars.

Dr Lumsden (Medical Officer of Health) and Nurse MacKay spent time in the school in January and February carrying out a programme of innoculation of children against diphtheria.

Miss Reid resumed duty in March after a month's absence because of illness. During this time Miss Mary MacKenzie had covered her classes.

Three pupils – evacuees from Glasgow – were enrolled on 23rd April but they did not remain long, returning to Glasgow on the 26th. Clydebank had been bombed on 13th March and many people, including children, were killed. The Log Book of Maryhill School in Glasgow noted that some of its pupils had been killed in the blitz. The situation in the Black Isle was very different. In spite of the proximity of Invergordon and its strategic port, there was little problem with German bombs. On one occasion it was reported in the *Ross-shire Journal* that the air-raid siren had sounded but the all- clear had come quickly.

In addition to having newspaper reports on the progress of the War, some people had a wireless. One girl recounted that their neighbours had boarded-out children living with them and so they had a wireless. She and her sisters and brothers used to go to the house, where they listened to the news. However, when they went home and their father asked them what it was they couldn't remember.

Fundraising

Children were always keen to collect for charitable causes and many of these collections were arranged through the school.

In May the sum of £2.16.8d (about £2.83 in today's money) was raised from the sale of 'Alexandra' Roses on behalf of the Royal Northern Infirmary, Inverness. RNI was then the main hospital in the town. The children's ward, not unknown to some of the local youngsters, was York Ward – opened by the King and Queen when they were Duke and Duchess of York.

The following month a sale of handwork made by Senior boys raised £1.12.6d. (£1.63) which was forwarded to the Scottish 'Penny-a-week' fund for the Red Cross. Earlier in the session a blanket knitted by senior girls had been given to the local branch.

In the *Ross-shire* on 19th September there was a report that Christobel Murray and Rosemary MacLeod had made a collection for the Scottish Children's League of Pity. The sum raised was £1.11s.7½d (£1.58).

The Poppy Day collection in November raised £2.1.8d (£2.08) which was sent to Edinburgh and in December £2 was sent to 'Penny-a-week' Headquarters for Mrs Churchill's 'Aid to Russia' Fund.

These may all seem like small amounts but in the early forties a couple could buy their week's groceries for less than £1 and an old-age pensioner received half that amount – ten shillings.

1941 - 42

In the Log Book there is a note at the beginning of October to the effect that ten bags of firewood were delivered to the school, followed by half a ton of coal on the next day. This was in preparation for the fire being lit around the middle of the month. Considering the size of the furnace and the number of radiators it had to heat this fuel would be unlikely to constitute the year's supply.

In October eight new dual desks were delivered. They had seats which tipped up and the desk lids lifted to reveal space underneath where the pupils could keep their books. There was a groove for

J. MacIver

pencils, a slot for slates and a hole for an inkwell. These desks were used until the middle of the sixties when they were replaced by modern tables and chairs.

We got our bible stories, we did our work
our sums, reading, spellings our sewing and
handy work, we sang and did our exercise too.
Outside we played around the great big tree,
Rounders, skipping, jumping and marbles what a skill.
When winter's snow and frost came we
slid and fell and slid again, we were
cold and wet, round the corner we did
have the biggest snowball fight and fun.
In spring time we had gym outside
and jumped and ran and raced.
It's time I said farewell, my eyes are
wet, I truly say I loved my teachers
friends and pals and Tore school, perhaps we
will meet up some other time.

Written in 1941 by Christobel Murray when she left Tore School.

The year 1942 saw the first launch of Germany's V2 rocket missile, designed by Wernher von Braun.

The issue of identity cards provided further evidence that the country was at the war. These cards had to be carried at all times and were to be in use until March 1952.

In attendance at the annual routine medical inspection in January with Dr Lumsden, was Nurse MacInnes who had newly arrived as District Nurse for the Parishes of Knockbain and Killearnan.

The MOH tested children's eyesight; the school dentist, Mr Ross, extracted teeth; and Mr MacKay of Glasgow Corporation called to interview boarded-out children.

In March 1942 the *Ross-shire* carried a notice from Dr George Thomson (Director of Education) regarding exemption from school for agricultural work. That was to be limited to those over twelve years of age, and no more than twenty attendances were to be missed except in emergencies. (Each day counted as two attendances.) No child was to work more than four hours each half day and no more than seven hours in a whole day. Eight weeks' holiday were to be fixed to suit agricultural needs.

On 3rd July the school closed for the summer holidays and Merit Certificates were awarded to pupils in all classes. That same month sweets and chocolate were added to the list of items rationed. Chocolate bars cost about 3½d (less than 5p).

1942 - 43

The school was closed for a Day of National Prayer on 3rd September, the third anniversary of the outbreak of the War. A similar day had been held in 1941 at the suggestion of the King. In this Parish a service was held at noon in the Free Church.

In March 1943 a representative of the Salvage Campaign Corps gave an interesting talk and showed photographs and a number of articles made from waste paper. The children were encouraged to collect paper. In March 1944 there was reference to this having raised 14s 4d which was put into the Red Cross box. Local people were saving all paper and putting it to the railway station (Allangrange) from where it was transported by train.

That year pupils who were members of the School Savings Group were asked to make a special effort for 'Wings for Victory' week. The target fixed for the group was £60. They did in fact save £155.15s and the number of contributors to the School Savings Group had doubled.

On 19th June Nurse MacInnes expressed satisfaction with the cleanliness of the children. The following week three cases of measles and two of jaundice were reported.

There continued to be frequent references to boarded-out children enrolling and leaving – to return to Glasgow or move to foster parents in another district. Some stayed a very short time while others spent their whole childhood with the same family and married and settled down, if not in the Black Isle, elsewhere in Ross-shire.

1943 - 44

The summer holidays of 1943 were short – five weeks – but a further month was to be given from 8th October for potato holidays.

Attendance Register

By 13th August, a week after school resumed, no registers or equipment had been received. The registers were the large blue books which had to be filled in, in ink, every day. When a child was absent 'o' was marked and when present 'x'. This was later simplified so that only the absences were recorded.

In the late eighties computerised records replaced these hand written registers.

Before the end of August a Ministry of Information van called at the school and 'a very interesting exhibition of films was given in the Public Hall'. This had been happening for the previous two years and continued to be a fairly regular occurrence several times a year. It would have been a treat for the children. The films produced by the Ministry of Information were related to the War.

In January 1944 the teacher sent in an application form for the issue of Wellington boots and in March seven pairs were given to the children who had bad roads to travel coming to school. Twenty-three ration coupons for these were sent by registered post to Miss Douglas, Maryburgh.

The Log Book contains the following note, written in February, concerning changes in the timetable for winter.

1942-43
a. Morning opening 10 am for whole school
b. Lunch interval 1 pm to 2 pm Infants 12.30
c.Morning interval 15 mins
d. Afternoon interval ——————
e. Total time in lessons Infants 195 mins Seniors 210 mins

Summer 1943
a. Morning opening 10 am
b. Lunch interval 1 pm to 2 pm Infants 12.30 pm
c. Morning interval 20 mins
d. Afternoon interval 10 mins
e. Total time in lessons Infants 210mins Seniors 270 mins
Winter 1943-44 as 42-43.

The change to the winter timetable took place on 22nd November and continued until the end of January. The school finished at 3.45 pm in winter and 4 pm in summer.

A 'Milk and Meals' Return form was received and a week later sent back to the Education Office. The idea of free milk dated back to1930 but there was no previous reference in the Log Book. Charles Fraser was the contractor for delivery. Neil Macleod remembers:

Free school milk was delivered and in the winter often froze and expanded into stalks of frozen milk that grew out of the top of the bottle pushing up the aluminium foil top.

The frozen milk on top tasted like ice-cream (or so we thought).

There were no school meals served in Tore until early 1956. The children who lived too far away to go home for dinner took a 'piece' and in the forties and fifties Neil's mother warmed up their tea or cocoa at the Schoolhouse Rayburn, just as the previous Headmaster's wife had done.

A Junior Red Cross Link was formed in the school in June with membership of twenty-five.

The 6th of June saw the start of the Normandy landings (D-Day) when one hundred and fifty-six thousand troops from Britain, USA and Canada were transported to Normandy to repel the German forces. This event was much celebrated and remembered in the year 2004.

The target for the Savings Group 'Salute to Soldiers' week was again £60 but reached £120.10/- which although an excellent effort was down on the previous year's amount.

1944 - 45

Only one month was allocated for the summer holidays, another month being given for 'potato holidays' in October /November. A week after school resumed in August two cases of dysentery were reported. During the week of 21st September Dr Horne, the new County MOH, made his first visit to the school and thirty children received treatment for immunisation against diphtheria.

In November £2.2s was sent to the Secretary of Junior Red Cross League for cigarettes for servicemen in hospital. In the light of today's attitude to smoking it is interesting to note how children were encouraged to raise money to buy cigarettes for men in hospital.

The school closed on 22nd December for Christmas with 'the usual party given by the teachers'.

In 1945 the post of Director of Education was officially created for each County Education Authority. Up until this time the County Clerk carried out the duty although Dr Thomson was frequently referred to as Director of Education.

For the first time transport was to be available for children under eight years of age who lived two miles or more from the school and for those over eight who lived more than three miles away.

At this time the school was used as a distribution point for orange juice and cod liver oil for children, the days for obtaining these being Monday and Thursday from 3.30 to 4 pm.

In March a box of gifts was received by the Junior Red Cross, for distribution. These were sent by the children of Mackinley School, Vallejo, California. A school of that name no longer exists in Vallejo.

The Alexandra Rose collection made by six of the school children in June raised £5.14. 9d. This was down a little on the previous year. The money was forwarded to RNI.

A letter was received from Mr Graham, Clerk to the School Management Committee, to say that for the Autumn holidays the school would close for three weeks at a time most suitable to the local farmers, but no further exemption would be granted after that time.

End of the War

On 8th May World War II in Europe ended in victory for Britain and her allies. This was known as VE day. The writer remembers her mother and grandmother putting up the celebration flags outside the house. Her father was stationed abroad at the time and was not to return home until 1946.

At the end of the month, on the afternoon of Saturday 28th May, the children were entertained to 'Victory' sports and tea. The sports were held in a field in front of the school – where houses have now been built. 'A committee of local ladies and gentlemen' were in charge and a very pleasant afternoon was spent. One local woman remembers attending this event with her small children.

During the war the ruling that married women could not be employed as teachers was in abeyance when so many male teachers were serving in the armed forces. In 1945 the disqualification was abolished altogether although even as late as the 1960s married women, returning to teaching after a break, were employed initially as non-permanent staff.

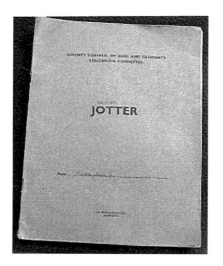 

Jotters and Exercise books all bore the logo, 'County Council of Ross and Cromarty Education Committee'. The back cover of jotters carried Arithmetical tables – measure, money, and multiplication tables up to twelve times table. Children were expected to know all these tables by heart and it was embarrassing to be caught consulting the back of the jotter.

9. The Post-War Age

1945 - 46

After the summer holidays the school reopened on 7th August with fifty children on the roll. Six pupils had gone on to secondary school and only one new infant was enrolled although two had already started at Easter.

Maureen Ross, Ishbel Cameron and Betty MacKinnon, the Qualifying Class of 1952.

This unusually small class proceeded through the school and, although personnel changed slightly, by 1951-52 when the qualifying class was reached there were still just three pupils.

On 15th and 16th August the school was closed for 'National Holidays' to celebrate the Japanese surrender (on 15th August) which ended World War II.

September of that year was a particularly bad month for the usual childhood illnesses – measles, whooping-cough, impetigo. The dates chosen, in consultation with local farmers, for the potato holidays were 28th September to 23rd October. When the school reopened there were four new pupils. This was a year which saw much movement of children. In May 1945 there had been sixty on the roll. By October that was down to fifty-four. A few months later, in March 1946, six boarded-out children left but shortly afterwards two children enrolled followed by a further six within a week.

Miss Gillies took charge of running the school on 30th November. Three weeks later, on 21st December, the Christmas holidays began. A *'Christmas tree and party for all the children'* was held that night in the Public Hall.

The school was to close for the Easter holidays on 11th April but the Headteacher was ill so it closed a week earlier. (Not much notice given there.) Classes resumed on the 15th and on the 19th six new pupils were admitted (probably infants) and two Glasgow boarded-out children left.

On 8th June Victory Day celebrations took the form of sports for the school children in the forenoon *'with liberal refreshments'* and in the afternoon the merit prizes for the year were presented. Each child also received a card signed by His Majesty King George.

Several problems were noted at this time concerning accommodation.

14th June   Lavatories choked. For several months a pane of glass in senior classroom window has been out, causing much discomfort. Repeatedly reported but nothing done.

There were more changes ahead after the summer holidays which had begun on 4th July.

On 20th August 1946 Norman Macleod, MA, a native of Lewis, took up duty as Headmaster. He came to Tore from Inverasdale, having also been employed for a time at Munlochy. He was married to Jean and they had two daughters, Christina and Dolleen, and one son, Neil, who as one of Her Majesty's Inspectors has been back to Tore School carrying out an inspection. Mr Macleod was a Gaelic speaker and talented singer.

It was not a very auspicious start for a new teacher. Miss Gillies, the assistant, was ill and so not present. One girl who had passed the Qualifying came back to school but then had to be sent elsewhere. Five new pupils were admitted – three from Arpafeelie (who went into Standard IV) and two Infants. The following day two pupils from the previous session returned putting the roll up to fifty-nine. A week later two boys arrived from Killearnan School without having changed their residence. This matter had to be reported to the Education Director and since such transference was not encouraged they were told, on his instructions, to return to Killearnan.

On 16th September the opening time of the school day was changed to 9.30 am instead of 10 am. About this time Avoch District School Management Committee (in whose area Tore was included) admitted they had made a mistake in dates and the holidays had been a week short. This was to be rectified in the autumn at the discretion of the Headmaster and in consultation with the farming community.

When the winter timetable went into operation in December the weather was boisterous and only thirty-two pupils were present.

School Christmas parties are remembered with nostalgia. They were held in Tore Hall and were open to all members of the community – parents, pre-school children, former pupils. Normal lessons were suspended for at least a day for the production of decorations – paper chains, lanterns and so on – for the Hall. The Milk Marketing Board supplied the shiny tinfoil strips out of which the milk bottle tops had been cut and when twisted lightly they made most attractive decorations. The huge (or so it seemed) Christmas tree came from the forest. Eggshells were painted to hang on the tree – no shiny baubles in those days. The 'snow' on the tree was cotton wool. The Hall looked wonderful by the time the teachers and children had finished.

> *I remember standing in awe gazing at the huge Christmas Tree on the corner of the stage and all the decorations and the 'buzz' that was around.*

The girls dressed up in their best frocks and the boys put on their suits and with Mums and Dads (sometimes) and Grannies and Grandas made their way to the Hall for 6.30 pm. Very few people had cars so most walked which was part of the fun.

The children provided entertainment – singing, Highland Dancing and a play. One girl remembers playing the Fairy Queen for which her mother created a 'make do and mend' costume of white satin material. There were games (mainly singing games with all the children joining in) and a delicious tea with sandwiches and cakes and biscuits. The highlight was the visit of Santa (a local farmer dressed up) with his reindeer (two other local men) pulling his cart. He gave all the children a *goodie* bag containing an apple and an orange and sweets. The Headmaster's family tell us that their father bought the sweets from Morganti and Simonelli, a well-known ice-cream shop in Dingwall. In the days of rationing the children brought him their sweets ration-coupons so that he could do this.

When school resumed in January 1947, after the Christmas break, coughs, colds and whooping cough reduced attendance to thirty-three (out of a roll of fifty-five).

The winter of 1946-47 was considered the coldest for over fifty years. Early 1947, 23rd January to 17th March, was characterised by very severe weather. On 28th February the Headmaster recorded, *'Snow was falling this morning and conditions were almost blizzard. Only 14 scholars attended and these were dismissed at 2 pm and two attendances marked.'* A week later he wrote,*'The snowstorm continued but does not affect attendance. Those who are absent say that illness or prolonged recovery is the cause.'*

On 13th March, in spite of the bad weather, Mr Murray HMI arrived to carry out an inspection. In his report, received in April, he commented on a shortage of class readers.

Big Room 1947

Back row: ? Kane, __, Ronnie Cameron, Willie MacKay, __.
Middle Row: Mr Norman MacLeod, John MacKay, ?Graham, Donnie Dalgetty, Alister MacRae, Peter Dalgetty, Bill Srail, Willie Johnstone, Billy Kane.
Front Row: Janette MacRae, Margaret Archibald, Ishbel MacRae, Betty Stewart, Jean MacKenzie (or Irvine), Molly Ferguson, Patsy Don, Dolly Ferguson, Margaret Mackenzie, Jasmine Fraser, __.

Later in the month a message was received to say that schools would close for the summer when the required number of openings (two hundred and three days) were attained and would open on 26th August. With school holiday dates now being planned more than a year ahead it is difficult to imagine not knowing until March when the school would be closed. Did the days of closure for snow count as openings or holidays?

Wee Room 1947

Back Row: Anthony Fraser, Jimmy Mellis, Norman Stevenson, Johnnie MacRae, Jackie MacRae, Iain MacLeod, Alec Sweeney.
2nd Row: James Graham, Eddie Fraser, David Sweeney, Duncan Hogg, Derek MacLeod, John Fraser, Brian Ross, Billy Wright, ? MacIver.
Front Row: __, Christina MacLeod, ___, Marion Oag, Marie MacRae, Pat Mellis, Maureen Ross, Lilian Hogg, Ishbel Hogg, Sandra Bain, Ishbel Cameron, Betty MacKinnon, Patty MacRae, ? MacIver

In April the school was closed for Easter holidays from 3rd to 14th. Eight infants were admitted after that.

The second annual Ross-shire Music Festival took place in Dingwall in early June. A choir of pupils from Tore took part on the 5th. This Festival was non-competitive although participants were adjudicated.

During the week of 20th June attendance was reduced by nearly half because of chickenpox and German measles.

1947 - 48

The summer of 1947 has gone down in history as one of the hottest and driest on record, after one of the severest winters on record. On Tuesday 26th August Mr Macleod wrote, 'School opened today after a glorious holiday of almost eight weeks with only one wet day.'

Nine pupils had left. Three had gone to Dingwall Academy and one to Munlochy Public School which still had a post-Primary department. What happened to the other five? Avoch Junior Secondary and Fortrose

Academy were possible destinations. Two infants were admitted bringing the school roll to fifty-five. Supplies of books and materials had not arrived, a situation which, although not unusual, must have been very frustrating for the teachers at the beginning of a new school year.

Early in October pupils were absent lifting potatoes. Of these, eight were under thirteen and were reported to the School Management Committee. One boy who was over thirteen was exempt. Two weeks later some were still absent without permission but just after that, on 27th October, the Headmaster wrote, *'Potato-lifters have taken a warning and returned to school except one boy who is employed lifting potatoes at home.'*

On November 5th the school closed for Harvest Thanksgiving and for two days mid-term holiday. Less than two weeks later there was a heavy fall of snow resulting in many children being absent.

For the occasion of the wedding of Princess Elizabeth (the present Queen), on 20th November, the school was closed. People listened to the wedding on the radio (no television then) trying to imagine what it was like there in London. One evening, at a later date, a film of the Royal wedding was included among others screened in the Hall. To little girls it was like watching a fairytale.

In 1947 the school leaving age was finally raised to fifteen and even then the possibility of putting it up to sixteen was being discussed.

The National Health Service was established in 1948 giving free medical treatment to everyone. On 15th April the school dentist extracted teeth and remarked that tooth decay was worse here than in other Black Isle schools. There was no speculation as to why this was so. The wells in this area produced 'hard' water reputed to be *'good for the teeth'* and this being a farming community, with plenty fresh milk, teeth should have been strong.

Generations of children hated the sight of the dentist's caravan parked at the side of the school. One former pupil remarked on the number of extractions which the dentists seemed to do.

A new feature was introduced in 1948 into the County Qualifying Examination for regulating the transfer of pupils from Primary school to Secondary. On 23rd April fourteen children in the senior classes sat an Intelligence Test – seven each of Class IV and the Qualifying class. That Test was to provide teachers with a measure of intelligence (IQ) of each pupil and was supposed to be helpful for the streaming process for Secondary School.

A few days later, on 26th April, the children were given an afternoon holiday in celebration of the King and Queen's silver wedding anniversary. We recall that in 1923 the school was closed on the day of their wedding.

At this time there were two visiting teachers: Mr Grant was itinerant Gymnastic Instructor coming to the school less than once per month. When he came took both rooms for Drill in the morning. The visiting Singing teacher was Miss MacKay but because she was ill Mr Curr, the County Music Organiser, trained a choir of senior pupils for the Music Festival which took place on 2nd June. Although the choir was not performing until 2.30 pm they had to leave the school at 11.30 am because of difficulty over transport. The Tore choir gained third place in the rural schools section, after Contin and Lochussie.

The day following the Festival was very wet. The children arrived at school with wet feet so they were allowed home at dinnertime and one attendance was recorded.

On 24th June the school was closed *'on the occasion of the King's visit to Inverness. A considerable number of the children wanted to go.'* The King and Queen were there for the Royal Highland Show. Crowds lined the pavement excitedly waiting for the royal car. After they had passed a wee boy wailed, *'Where's the King and Queen?'* He had been looking for crowns and robes.

The first Olympic Games since 1936 were held in 1948. Britain was the host nation for the first time in forty years and British athletes won four silver medals.

1948 - 49

When the school resumed after the holidays three pupils had left for Fortrose Academy, two for Avoch Junior Secondary School, two for Dingwall Academy and one had moved from the district. Four infants had enrolled and the school roll was up to sixty-two.

In November Dr Horne (School Medical Officer) innoculated forty-five children against diphtheria and some against whooping cough. Some of these children were pre-schoolers. The following day in school some of the pupils were suffering the effects of the injection. A second dose of vaccine was given about a month later.

At the end of the month, with the shortening day, the dinner hour was reduced to half an hour and school closed in the afternoon at 3.30. Electricity had still not arrived in the area.

After the Christmas holidays Mrs Down, from Fortrose, took up duty as Singing teacher in the school. Her first visit was on 10th January 1949.

On 23rd January, as the days lengthened, normal timetable was resumed. Because of high winds and snow on 11th February several pupils who went home at dinnertime did not return. A week later a family was sent home because their young brother had scarlet fever. They were absent from school for a month.

For some unknown reason Tore opened a day earlier than other schools after Easter and as a result no milk was delivered that day.

In April 1949 notification was made to Secondary Schools that children who attained the leaving age of fifteen by Easter could leave school at that time. From then until the early 1970s Easter was a popular leaving date.

At the Music Festival in Dingwall a girl soloist competed on the 1st of June and the following day a choir of nineteen children, conducted by Mrs Down, gained first place out of seven schools in their class (for one and two-teacher schools).

1949 - 50

After an excellent summer of sunshine the school opened on 23rd August with the weather still bright and dry. There were fifty-five children on the roll (twenty-six of whom were boys). Six pupils had gone to Dingwall Academy.

At this time there was an element of choice of Secondary School depending on where the children lived. If they were on a bus route to Dingwall (and most were) they were permitted to attend there. Dingwall Academy provided education for all levels of ability regardless of Qualifying Examination results. Some chose Avoch School since there was a more suitable bus going in that direction. Transport for Fortrose Academy was more difficult and a taxi had to take the pupils to Munlochy to catch a bus arriving in Fortrose in time for school opening.

In the early 1970s, with the provision of comprehensive education and the ending of the Qualifying examination, Avoch School lost its Junior Secondary status and became Primary only. All who would have gone to Avoch for Secondary education were directed to Fortrose. Some Tore children of the 1970s attended Dingwall Academy but by 1980 the school was firmly within the Fortrose Academy catchment area. Later in the 1980s, under the terms of the Parents' Charter, families could choose their children's school but transport outwith the catchment area was at their own expense.

On 9th September 1949 senior pupils were taken by the Headmaster to an Exhibition of Pottery in the old Academy Buildings in Dingwall. They left by bus at 11.15 am and returned at 1.30 pm. Miss Gillies conducted the rest of the school.

Early in October while Miss Gillies was absent, singing with the Dingwall Gaelic choir at the Inverness Mod, Miss Murray, the sewing Inspectress, arrived. She did not wait since Miss Gillies, who taught the girls needlework, was away.

In December there was a visit from HMI Mr Murray who examined the classes in the assistant's room and spent a short time in the Headmaster's room. He returned in March 1950 to examine Classes 2 to 5. A report received later that year indicated improvement in several areas of work and a very favourable comment on the building. *The school premises are in very good order, being well lighted, well heated comfortable and clean. The cleaner deserves a word of praise.'* Mrs Henderson, who lived in the village, was the school cleaner then.

In January 1950 the weather was mild for the time of year – a change from the severe storms which were usually a feature of the early part of the year.

10. Memories of the Fifties

The children of the fifties were too young to have any but hazy recollections of the War. For them life was more carefree and many happy memories stand out. Several have shared their reminiscences.

Memories

> *In spring and summer we had lots of fun climbing a big tree in the wood behind the schoolhouse. There were seasons of Hide and Seek, often played around the area of the hall, and Hoist the Flag. The latter was played with two teams one of which went to hide. A representative came back and on the ground drew out a complicated map of where they were hiding. The challenge to the opposing team was to find them before someone from the team in hiding rushed back to the den to hoist the flag.*
>
> *When winter with its frost and snow came we used to cross the road into the wood where the houses are now. There was a steep bank with a hollow where lying water froze. It made a great slide. We'd spend the whole interval there until we heard the bell and then raced back. There was no lining up so it was straight in to lessons. At lunchtime we'd rush our lunch (a piece and a warm drink) and head down to the curling pond which had a small 'overflow pond'. There was plenty scope there for slides and we never needed to be warned of the dangers of ice.*
>
> *What freedom we had then when we could roam at will over the countryside. The school gate was never shut.*

There was the season of marbles (for the boys), hopscotch or skipping for the girls. Skipping was accompanied by rhymes.

The girls also played a ball game against the end wall of the school with a series of actions before catching the ball as it came down. They chanted the action, *'Plainie, clappie, rollie, backie, right hand, left hand, touch your heel, touch your toe, touch the ground, birlie round.'*

'Plainie' meant a throw and catch. 'Clappie' meant clapping hands before catching the ball. 'Rollie' – roll arms; 'backie' – clap hands behind the back and so on.

Handball was one of the formal games played as part of the 'Drill' class. The trees at each side of the playground formed the goals. Handball, incidentally, is now a popular Olympic sport. One former pupil refuted the suggestion that this game originated in Tore!

During the Spring and Summer months Nature Study featured in the curriculum. On a good day we were sent out to pick wildflowers (what would the conservationists say?) and then returned to the classroom to try to identify them. Some conscientious pupils brought jars of frogs' spawn (*'jelly'*) from the curling pond and they stood on the window sill until tadpoles appeared. *'We were never told what happenend after that.'*

One of the highlights of the week was when the Headmaster read to the pupils. Favourites were *Kidnapped* and *Uncle Tom's Cabin* while *David Copperfield* made an impression on one pupil who used to compare the teacher to one of the characters in the book. Mr Macleod's talents as an actor came through as he brought the books alive with his expressive reading. Sometimes he had to stop because of the effect on himself of an emotive passage. Elspeth Oag (Mrs Skrodzka) believes that her love of literature can be traced back to those days.

Up until the early fifties library books came from Dingwall in large wooden boxes. When the period of loan was over the pupils helped check them by having a pile each as the teacher called out the titles. Then a library van began to come round every few months and the children were taken out to select books for the school library. There was a distinctive smell in that van – like perfume. Was it simply a blend of old and new books?

Memorising poetry was encouraged and some people can still after all those years churn out *Daffodils* by Wordsworth or *The Landing of the Pilgrim Fathers* by Hemans. Pupils were given the opportunity to write their own poems but within severe restrictions of metre and rhyme. Alas, Tore failed to produce a Wordsworth or a Betjeman.

Because school trips were infrequent they were memorable. One such excursion was to Inverness, across on the ferry from North Kessock. Transport to Kessock was on Archie's bus – a regular service between Kessock and Dingwall operated by Archie MacRae from the mid 1920s to the1960s.

We walked into the town, stopping at the harbour to watch boats being unloaded and then on to the Museum. At another time we went to Rosemarkie where we explored the beach and the caves. We discussed shells and stones and guddled in rock pools disturbing small sea creatures who were taking refuge there.

Culloden Moor was another area of interest. It was not, in the fifties, as highly developed a tourist attraction as it is today: the visitor centre did not exist and the main road passed in front of the cairn. There are memories of long walks during these trips. In a day when many children walked considerable distances to school this presented little problem.

Our recollection of Geography and History is that we spent a lot of time studying Scotland and England. There were large colourful maps hanging on the classroom wall from which we memorised the counties of Scotland starting with Shetland in the North and finishing with Wigtownshire in the South. Trying to remember the English counties was much more difficult.

Sums were done from *Holmes Comprehensive Arithmetic* which some pupils liked and they competed with each other to be ahead. Others hated the series. They were certainly not exciting books – with not one picture just pages of sums.

Mr Campbell was Art Organiser and he paid occasional visits to the school but otherwise the teacher conducted the lesson. For some, memories of Drawing lessons are not very happy ones. Nothing ever seemed to go right.

Sometimes we copied the pictures which hung on the walls – 'A Boy with A Rabbit' and a shepherd boy praying were favourites – of the teacher if not of the pupils. At other times we drew (or painted) the view from the classroom windows. It was a spectacular view stretching to the Monadhliadh Mountains. In Spring when the fields were being ploughed we could watch a patchwork emerging.

The view from the windows has now been almost completely obscured by houses.

The pictures mentioned were received from the Medici Society in 1937 and the one of the shepherd boy was called, *'He Prayeth Best who Loveth Best.'*

1950 - 51 Changes

After ten years at the school Donella Gillies left in June 1950 to take up an appointment in the Primary Department of Dingwall Academy. She remained there until she retired. Miss Gillies died in 1997 at the age of eighty-six.

Rena Cadger, MA, whose home was at Allanglach, took up duty at Tore in August, having come from the Royal School of Dunkeld in Perthshire.

That first day Miss Cadger rode into the playground on her bike. The children were all curious – a new teacher was a big change in the life of small children. In addition to having responsibility for teaching the pupils in the first three classes (the wee room) she took the older girls for Needlework – sewing and knitting – an arrangement which continued for two years until a specialist teacher was appointed.

Margaret Fraser (now Mrs Steven) was a member of Miss Cadger's first Primary 1 class in Tore. Margaret's grandfather, John Fraser, mason, had been involved in the reconstruction of the school in 1936 and was probably also responsible for carting the stones for the playground in 1931. Her own family, Leslie and Lorraine, were pupils in the school in the 1970s. Margaret's father is in the 1927 football photograph.

In 1950 the Free Church started a Sunday School which was held in the school. The Headmaster was the Superintendent and there were two other teachers. A large number of children from the locality attended whether or not their family was connected to the Free Church.

It was around this time that electricity came to Tore and the school was wired up with power. An electric pump was installed to replace the hand pump in the boys' cloakroom. This new pump was situated in the end room, near the far window, right above the well.

In the autumn school children were encouraged to gather rosehips (or *muckans* as they were known locally) for the production of rosehip syrup – an excellent source of vitamin C and acceptable alternative to citrus fruits which had not been available during the war. The fact that they were paid for what they picked was a great incentive for the children. Wild roses grew in profusion by the roadside and flowered prolifically over the summer so there was no lack of fruit. Bags were very quickly filled and taken to school and from there despatched by the Headmaster to the railway station.

That year as early as 1st December there was enough snow falling to justify foregoing the lunch break and sending the pupils home early. This was followed by low temperatures in January when ice formed on the playground and the children found places to make slides.

Early in 1951 there was a 'flu epidemic and many chidren were affected. The Black Isle Notes in the *Ross-shire Journal* of 5th January contained a reference to the fact that Fortrose and District was *'in the grip'* of flu over the New Year period.

The children of Tore, Killearnan, Arpafeelie, Drumsmittal and Upper Knockbain schools were entertained on Friday 5th January to a picture show with a varied programme, in Tore Hall. Mr and Mrs MacIver, Kilcoy Mains, provided each child with a bag of pears and apples (from their own productive orchard).

During 1950-51 the designation of classes as Lower and Higher Infants and Standard I to V was disposed of and replaced by Class I to VII which within a year became Primary I to VII, a term which has lasted.

Norman Macleod was very keen on Drama and in addition to being involved with the local Drama group he produced plays with the school children. These were performed either at the Christmas party or at a concert arranged later in the year. One parent remembers being impressed by Alistair (Sandy) Jack's performance of a cobbler.

In March 1951 the Qualifying Exam for Primary VII was held over two days, Arithmetic in the morning of the first day and English – Dictation, Grammar and Composition – in the morning of the second day. The supervisors were Mrs Ballingall on the first day and her husband on the second. Mr Ballingall was minister in the Church of Scotland. During the previous week Intelligence Tests were given to the top two classes.

The Headmaster recorded one day in April that the weather was so *'boisterous'* that children could not go home at the dinner interval and so school was continued till 2 pm and then the pupils were sent home. There was no record of parents being informed of this change. (No telephones.) Perhaps some sort of 'bush telegraph' went into operation but since mothers were generally at home all day there was unlikely to be a problem.

In June 1951 war broke out in Korea and British troops were drafted to assist. It was to last two years. On June 6th a choir which had been trained by Mr Curr the County Music Organiser competed in the Music Festival in Dingwall. It was conducted by Miss Cadger because Mrs Down, the Singing teacher, had been absent for some time due to illness.

Choir 1951
Photograph: F.W. Urquhart

Back Row: Johnnie MacRae, David Sweeney, John Fraser, Lilian Hogg, Janette MacRae, Marie MacRae, Mary Noble.
2nd Row: Calum Fraser, Norman Stevenson, Marion Oag, Christina Macleod, Elspeth Oag, Ishbel Cameron, Yvonne Adams, Ishbel Hogg.
Front Row: Alec Sweeney, Neil MacFarlane, Isobel Dalgetty, Jean MacFarlane, Dolleen Macleod, Cath MacLean, Patty MacRae, Betty MacKinnon.

The usual Bible Knowledge examination at the end of the term was conducted by Rev R. J. Murray, Free Church minister.

For the daily Religious Instruction lesson Mr Macleod very often read large chunks of the Bible while the children followed in their school Bibles. He had a habit of suddenly pouncing on someone. *'What's the next word?'* Almost invariably this was to someone who wasn't giving the matter full attention and woe betide the one who was caught out. Sometimes he asked a pupil to read. A girl of the time remembers her embarrassment after reading, 'He girded up his lions,' thinking that the word 'loins' was a misprint.

Extensive pieces of memory work had to be learned including answers to questions from *The Shorter Catechism*. In October 1950 an amended Religious Instruction Syllabus for Ross-shire schools was published. It included details of which Catechism answers were to be learned by each class from Primary III to Secondary II. Answers to all one hundred and seven Questions would be memorised over those seven years.

School Sports Day

Each year, towards the end of June, sports were held either in MacLennans' field beside the school or in the nearby football field. There were races for all age groups – flat race, egg and spoon race, high jump, three legged race, sack race and the whole event was great fun. Sometimes the money left over from the Christmas Treat was used as prizes. Good athletes could add considerably to their holiday spending money. First prize was one shilling, second was sixpence and third was a threepenny bit. A shilling in 1951 had the buying power of £1 (or more) of today's money.

On one occasion there were inter-school sports with Killearnan School. Since the latter was, by that time, a very small school the Tore pupils had no difficulty in winning.

Junior Classes
1951-52

Back Row: Maxwell MacPhee, Victor Cameron, Johnny MacKay, Sandy Jack, Martin MacLean, Neil Macleod, Sandy Rose.
2nd row: Tommy Adams, Ian Bain, Marlene Dalgetty, Cath MacLean, Doris Hogg, Duncan Cameron, Willie Davidson.
Front row: __. Catherine Cameron, Mary Sloan, Nancy MacKay, Naomi Dalgetty, Miriam Ahmed, Margaret Fraser, Rosemary MacKintosh, __.

A New Elizabethan Age

1951-52

For the first part of this session the pupils were dogged by poor health. There were two cases of appendicitis in the early months. In the New Year one child suffered pneumonia and there were many cases of unusual colds.

The Black Isle Railway closed to passengers on 1st October 1951. An increase in the number of bus services, and the fact that many families were acquiring cars, accelerated its demise.

On 6th February 1952, Miss Cadger answered a knock on the staffroom door at dinnertime. A little boy from Primary 3 was standing there and he announced, 'The King is dead'. King George VI had died and his daughter, Princess Elizabeth, was now Queen. Although on the day of the previous King's funeral in 1936 the children had been given a holiday this was not the case in 1952. The school was open as usual but all the classes gathered together in one room, shortly before the observance of a minute's silence, to listen to the radio broadcast.

Senior Classes 1951-52

Back Row: Ian MacLeod, Evan Smith, Christina Macleod, Mairi Adams,Betty MacKinnon, Norman Stevenson, John Jack, Mr Norman Macleod.
2nd row:Jackie MacRae, Patty MacRae,Yvonne Adams, Jane Urquhart, Ishbel Cameron, Marie MacRae, Maureen Ross, Ishbel Hogg, Sandra Bain, Johnnie MacRae.
3rd row: Mary Gallacher, Jean MacFarlane, Shona MacKintosh, Isobel Dalgetty, Elspeth Oag, Marion Oag, Dolleen Macleod, Florence Urquhart, Katie MacKay.
Front Row: Alec Sweeney, Neil MacFarlane, Joe Davidson, Calum Fraser, Anthony Fraser, Roddy MacRae, Kenny MacLennan.

In September Donald Patience, a Gym teacher based at Dingwall Academy, joined the staff in Tore as teacher of Drill. He visited the school every alternate Monday and on the weeks when he was not there the teachers carried out the work. The lessons took place in the playground.

Miss Lydia Munro, a qualified teacher of Needlework, arrived in October and taught the girls every Friday afternoon. There were no sewing machines – every stitch was done by hand. Miss Munro belonged to Alness but worked in Avoch Junior Secondary School where she also taught Cookery. While the girls were doing Needlework the Headmaster took the boys for Handwork using mainly cane and raffia. The basketwork was of a particularly high standard and some is still in existence. Lower primaries made cane and raffia tablemats and progressed to basketmaking in the upper classes. One year the senior boys made willow baskets from branches cut locally, similar to the creels used by fishermen in Mr Macleod's native Lewis.

In-service days were very uncommon but Miss Cadger attended a course of instruction organised by Mr Curr for the teaching of Singing. She helped train the school choir between visits from the Singing teacher.

After an inspection by HMI Mr Murray in January 1953 the school received a very good report. The premises were described as modern and the classrooms bright, clean and comfortable. We remember that the building underwent an extensive renovation sixteen years previously. Good progress was reported in most subjects in both classrooms.

A group at Redcastle on Coronation Day

In June, sixteen months after the death of her father, the new Queen was crowned. Three days of holiday were granted, 1st to 3rd June, in celebration of this event. On the morning of Coronation Day, 2nd June, the news broke that New Zealander Edmund Hillary and Sherpa Tenzing Norgay, members of a British expedition, had on 29th May reached the top of Mount Everest, the first people to do so.

To celebrate the Coronation the children of the Parish were entertained to sports and a party at Redcastle. From the field where the event took place they marched, waving their flags, to the Castle.

As they stood on the lawn Baroness Burton and other dignitaries came out on to the castle balcony.

In commemoration of the Coronation each child received a New Testament and a mug.

Later in the month they were all bussed to Inverness to see a film of the Coronation.

A week later the Music Festival took place in Dingwall and the Tore School choir gained second place in their class (two-teacher schools).

Mrs Down conducting
and to the right the Choir

For a short time in 1951 sweets had been unrationed but the demand became so great that they were soon rerationed. It was 1953 before they could finally be bought without coupons. On the morning in which this was actioned one of the older girls rushed into the classroom as the pupils were gathering. She had a handful of sweets which she shared out to everyone. Most of the children didn't know until then that they could buy unlimited amounts of sweets. Fortunately for their teeth they didn't have the money to buy unlimited amounts.

William Golding published *Lord of the Flies* in 1953 and thirty years later he received the Nobel Prize for Literature.

Roger Bannister, an English athlete, ran a mile in under four minutes – the first person to do so.

1953-54

Mr Macleod loved to tease his pupils with riddles. *'Which is heavier a ton of bricks or a ton of feathers?'* (As if anyone would want a ton of feathers.) Most of the children fell into the trap.

In November 1953 Mrs Henderson who had been school cleaner for more than eight years gave up the position. In tribute, the Headmaster wrote,

'She was an ideal servant who knew her job and did it. While she was here there was no fault to be found with the cleaning of the school,' and there were references in HMI reports to the cleanliness of the school. The Headmaster's wife took on the cleaning until Mrs MacKinnon was appointed. They both kept up the extremely high standard.

Throughout January 1954 attendance was poor because of an epidemic of colds and flu.

Tempest Photography

1954

Back Row: Virginia Fraser, Catherine Cameron, Sandy Rose, Victor Cameron, Martin MacLean, Miriam Ahmed, Barbara Urquhart, Margaret Fraser, Mary Sinclair, Mary Sloan, Willie Davidson, Johnny MacKay, Neil Macleod, Rosemary MacKintosh, Violet MacKay.
2nd row: Kenny MacLennan, Maxwell MacPhee, Roddy MacRae, Tommy Adams, Joe Davidson, Ian Bain, Norman Stevenson, David Sinclair, Calum Fraser, John Jack, Frank Davidson, Anthony Fraser, Neil MacFarlane, Duncan Cameron, Sandy Jack.
Seated: Naomi Dalgetty, Doris Hogg, Jean MacFarlane, Sandra MacRae, Dolleen Macleod, Christina Macleod, Miss Rena Cadger, Mr Norman Macleod, Elspeth Oag, Sandra Bain, Cath MacLean, Isobel Dalgetty, Marlene Dalgetty, Katie MacKay, Nancy MacKay.
Front Row: Danny Adams, Anne Gordon, Irene Hogg, John Rose.

A very good report in Religious Instruction for the previous session was received in February. Questions were answered correctly, repetition of Metrical Psalms was almost perfect and repetition of the Shorter Catechism excellently done. It was noted under 'Singing' that the work of the day began with praise and prayer and at the close of the examination the children sang Psalm 23 to the tune 'Crimond'. The Minister was impressed. Also under scrutiny was the topic of temperance – the answers which the children gave to the questions indicated that they were sufficiently instructed in that subject.

A pupil from an earlier time remembered her class having a talk on alcohol, possibly by a member of a group known as the Band of Hope who were invited into schools.

> *We didn't know what alcohol was. If they'd said 'whisky' we'd have known. Then we had to do a composition and one boy wrote, 'Alcohol affects your barn.'*

It is significant that allowance was made in the report for the inspection of Gaelic although there was nothing to report from Tore. The language had almost died out in this area with only a few older members of the community being fluent speakers. At this time the Island of Lewis where Gaelic was (and still is) widely used was part of Ross and Cromarty, and much of Wester Ross was also Gaelic-speaking.

A few days before school closed for the summer holidays in 1954 there was an eclipse of the sun. For the youngsters it was their first experience of this phenomenon and they were taken outside to watch it through glass which had been blackened with candle smoke. The eerie darkness which descended about mid-day made an impression on them.

1954 - 55

In 1954 Arpafeelie School closed and its catchment area was divided between Tore, Drumsmittal and Munlochy Schools. Eleven pupils were transferred to Tore.

Around this time a filmstrip/slide projector arrived in the school. This piece of equipment was eagerly received – in those days before TV and video.

In the latter quarter of 1954 epidemics of mumps and chickenpox raged in the area among children of all ages. In addition, towards the end of the year, a flu epidemic set in. Attendance reached its lowest for many years with more than half the children absent just before Christmas. The school party was postponed for about a week.

After the Christmas holidays attendance was not much better and a January snowstorm meant even fewer pupils in school. The winter of 1955 is well remembered in the area. There were drifts of two to three feet blocking the roads so that schools were closed and people could not go to work.

This scenario was repeated in February when severe snowstorms again blocked roads. An eyewitness account of 17th February informed,

> *Last night much snow fell and has been piled up in drifts by high wind. This morning was a terrifying day for children with a blizzard from the east.*

The *Ross-shire Journal* of 25th February reported on the storm, describing it as the worst for sixty years. On Wednesday 16th there were *'heavy falls of snow drifting before a wind of gale force. All Wednesday night, all next day and the greater part of the night.'*

In places there were drifts up to twenty feet and two trains (with sixty passengers) were stuck in Alness. A helicopter had to be sent to pick up a doctor to attend a patient in the Black Isle. The schools were closed for two days, buses were stuck and the mail was disrupted. On 22nd and 23rd the severest frost of the century was recorded.

127

On 12th April 1955 the vaccine against polio which had been discovered by Jonas Salk went on sale. Just prior to this the incidence of polio worldwide peaked. About a year later the first vaccinations were being administered in Tore – to pre-school children. Polio was a serious illness which could cause paralysis and was feared by adults and children. With the use of the vaccine the number of reported cases declined rapidly and by 2004 there were fewer than nine hundred known cases in the whole world.

At the Music Festival in June the school choir, conducted by Mrs Gray, was placed third out of nine, only two marks behind the winning choir.

Mrs Cecilia Gray had been appointed music teacher at the beginning of the session. She is referred to in 1927 when, as Miss Cecilia Murray, she undertook teaching practice in the school. On qualifying she had worked as an assistant teacher at Drumsmittal School until her marriage to Dr James Gray the GP in Munlochy.

Choir 1956
with Miss Cadger

At the same Festival Sandra MacRae, a pupil in Primary 7, gained first place in piano solo for 11-13 year-olds. Sandra went on to study at the Royal Scottish Academy of Music in Glasgow and then at Glasgow University where she gained a degree in music. Following that she qualified as a Music Teacher.

Early in 1955 discussions were being held with the prospect of school meals being provided. Mr May who was HMI called in connection with alterations to the spare classroom to convert it to a dining room.

In July notice was given that 'Equal Pay' for women teachers was to be implemented by 1961. At that time the starting salary for a teacher was £407 per year. The train fare from Dingwall to Aberdeen cost 24s (£1.20).

1955 - 56

The summer of 1955 was reminiscent of that of 1947 – another of the hottest on record after an exceptionally severe winter. In the village and surrounding area wells ran dry and tanks of water had to be brought in. These were sited at the garage and residents went along with pails to collect their supply. Some locals even went to the Clootie Well near Munlochy to fetch water. This drought accelerated the provision of the Black Isle water scheme bringing water from Loch Glass, near Evanton.

In September, three weeks into the school term, Jean Murray from the Free Church Manse spent two weeks on teaching practice in preparation for her course in Edinburgh.

That same month the telephone came to homes in Tore. Until then calls could be made only from the (red) Kiosk which, along with the letterbox, stood at the foot of the smiddy brae. The phone number was Tore 1, shared with the Post Office which was located at Allangrange Station. There was no direct dialling but all calls went through an operator (usually a woman) who told the caller how much to put in the box. On connection she advised, 'Press Button A'. If the connection could not be made it was, 'Press Button B' (and the caller's money was returned). When the telephone was installed in homes all numbers, including the Kiosk and Post Office, were connected to the Munlochy exchange. There were shared party lines which meant that, when the receiver was picked up, if the other family was using the telephone their conversation could be heard. That unsatisfactory arrangement was necessary because of a shortage of lines. The writer's family shared a line with the schoolhouse.

That term Miss Joan Penny from Fortrose spent some time in Tore as Singing teacher in the absence of Mrs Gray.

On February 22nd school dinners were supplied for the first time. Mrs MacKinnon, the school cleaner, was appointed to serve the meals which were prepared in the canteen at Munlochy School and transported to Tore. It was a great novelty having dinner in school. The writer along with her friend, Betty MacKinnon, helped Betty's mother wash dishes in preparation for that day.

Norman Macleod left Tore in March to take up an appointment in Aberdeen as teacher of Mathematics at Northfield School. Miss Cadger was appointed interim Head until a new Headteacher could take up duty. Miss Grace MacNab, a teacher at Drumsmittal School, came to assist her.

Mr Macleod remained in Northfield until his retirement in 1968. He died on 6th February 1994 at the age of eighty-five.

In June 1956 the Royal Highland Show was again held in Inverness. Miss Cadger and Miss MacNab took a group of the older children to the Show in the afternoon — after school.

This was a year of crisis over the use

of the Suez Canal, triggering the threat of another World War with the added fear that nuclear weapons would be used, similar to those which devastated Hiroshima and Nagasaki in Japan in 1945. Petrol had to be rationed and as a result learner drivers were allowed to drive unaccompanied. In December Anglo-French forces evacuated the Canal which had been blocked to Western shipping and the crisis was over.

New Headmaster

1956 - 57

Mr Alasdair U. Mackenzie, MA, from Cromarty Junior Secondary School, took up duty as Headmaster at the beginning of the session and Grace MacNab returned to Drumsmittal.

Mr Mackenzie has written some recollections of his time as Headteacher in Tore School.

I was Headmaster at Tore School from 1956 – 1963 and during these years I was fortunate to have the services of Rena Cadger as my Assistant.

The roll during these years was generally in the mid-fifties but for a short spell it was over sixty, which entitled us to a third teacher, who was Mrs MacFarquhar.

Arpafeelie School had not long closed and pupils had transferred to Tore. The younger pupils, up to eight years, were transported by taxi – Jock Hutcheson from the Artafallie

Four sets of twins

Stores. The older pupils walked or cycled. There were three sets of twins at the Infant end of the School at that time – two boys, George and Maitland Jack, from Woodend, two girls Pamela and Patricia Dalgetty and another two girls, Sandra and Joan Mackenzie, whose father was "Alick the Busdriver".

During these years there were several "Boarded Out" pupils on the Roll but their numbers were dwindling rapidly. There was also an encampment of travelling people in the area and we had several pupils from there.

As to the special events my memory is somewhat blurred. I

Pupils and staff at Cromarty.
The tall lady is Miss Munro, sewing teacher.

can recall a School Trip to Cromarty in May 1957 to see the Royal Yacht Britannia – with the Queen on board – sailing up to Invergordon.

I can also recall visits to Culloden and to the Museum in Inverness and of course visits to Music

Festivals, where the pupils acquitted themselves very creditably. For the first two to three years of my time at Tore, the School and Schoolhouse water supply came from a well beneath the School and there was an electric pump which I had to switch on from time to time. We did eventually get a Mains water supply and at the same time the old coal fired stove, which incidentally I had to light and stoke each morning, was replaced by an oil-fired furnace – we were creeping into the 20th century.

I must say my time at Tore School was a happy one. The pupils were courteous, friendly and well-behaved; and amongst them there was a fair sprinkling of very able children.

Mr Mackenzie's daughter, Mairi Strachan, who was a pupil from 1958 to 1963 has written some of her childhood memories.

I was a baby when our family moved to the Tore Schoolhouse in '56. Tore School was my first School and also my Nursery School – unusual in those days —as apparently I disappeared one day (around age three) and my mother finally found me – sitting with my arms folded – in the front row of P1! From that day I attended School, coming and going at will. I started officially on my fourth birthday – in floods of tears as I could no longer go home when I felt like it.

I seem to recall in those days that the early stage P1s finished at lunch-time, the next stage at 3 pm: but all who had to wait for a taxi just remained in the playground until it arrived for the 'big ones' at 4 pm. I lived on the School premises so this meant an afternoon of playmates for me! In extreme weather we repaired to the cloakrooms where we used the coat hooks as an unofficial gym – scaling them from one end to the other without touching the ground and hanging upside-down and swinging from them by our feet – our heads dangling above the concrete floor below!

The events I particularly recall were the School Christmas Parties in the Tore Hall, attended by mothers, grannies and younger siblings. This was a day for frilly frocks for the girls and ties (and kilts for some) for the boys – for an afternoon of Pass the Parcel, The Grand Old Duke of York and other games. Santa always attended which was a huge event. I seem to recall a School Concert being staged in the Hall too. This may have

131

been at night which would have made it a momentous occasion for us. I played a Daisy in a musical dancing piece, and I recall an older class singing something incredibly glamorous with shadow puppets. One big event for me was attending the evening Christmas Party my father put on for previous years' Leavers, each year. These ex-pupils seemed very grown-up and sophisticated to me – in party gowns and suits – and any staff connected with the School were invited also. I remember everybody dancing the "Twist" which was in vogue at the time and having mince pies and School custard at the end of the evening.

Gym was held in the Tore Hall also and was known as 'drill' originally! When Jock Watt, the dashing new Gym teacher, arrived it became Gym and the girls were instructed to wear shorts – which was unheard of then as shorts were only for the beach and the summer holidays.

We had long playtimes then: 30 minutes at 11 am, 60 minutes at 'dinner-time' and 15 minutes at 3 pm The ritual after lunch, which was cooked at Munlochy and served on the premises by Mrs MacKinnon, was for all the children to head down to Mrs Kirk's Sweetie Shop for the highlight of the day – a Tobermory Tattie, a penny chew or a sherbert chew, McCowan's toffee, a sherbert fountain – endless choices. At playtimes we ranged far and wide – into the woods behind the school, into and under the whins around the Hall and across the adjoining the fields, especially in winter and spring – for sliding on the ice and then looking for tadpoles later on. We also made frequent forays down the 'Bumpy Road' collecting wild rasps, brambles and rose hips etc depending on the season.

Other than a visiting Gym Teacher we had Mrs Gray for music each week. She always wore exotic dangly earrings and I recall seeing them at very close quarters once as I had to sit on her knee while she played the piano for the class singing. This was probably before I had started School proper to keep me still! We had periodical visits from the Rev Richard Bolster for our religious and moral instruction. I remember he kept us guessing for ages on the riddle of the oldest thing in the world. Having exhausted rocks, dinosaurs and so on we were a little disappointed and puzzled to discover it was in fact Love. We never had a visiting Art Teacher but in Miss Cadger's class I remember regular art projects and even taking a turn painting with big brushes on an easel which was a huge thrill. Looking back I can see what a fantastic teacher she was – far from just the three Rs we did drama, art, nature study etc. There was also a big cupboard full of exciting jigsaw puzzles, books, plasticene and so on which we could dip into when we'd finished our work. A big highlight for us was the occasional use of the Projector; it was almost as thrilling as a trip to the Pictures – to see the blackout blinds coming down and hear the machine whirring into life.

I remember attending the County Music Festival in Dingwall with my classmates and being involved in choirs and choral and solo verse speaking. There was no School uniform then but everyone wore kilt and tie to attend. This was an extremely rigorous and serious affair with much rehearsing beforehand and detailed assessments from the Judges afterwards.

Looking back things were physically quite primitive. In the winter the heating could be quite inadequate first thing in the morning and I remember the whole class having to do warmup exercises before lessons started. The free milk was at room temperature so was either lukewarm or half frozen (a special treat). The School toilets were in a separate open air building across the playground and at one point there was still an open 'midden' for rubbish and canteen refuse at the back of the school: this was later filled in and became a sand-pit.

I remember one winter the snow being so deep that my father had to dig us out of our back door. Only about seven pupils made it in to School that day: this small group of us endeavoured to drink the entire milk delivery, which was all delightfully half-frozen. On this or perhaps another occasion a severe blizzard raged and I remember my father closing the school and running pupils home to remote crofts in his car. I accompanied him on this highly exciting mission.

After the October break of 1956, which had extended to a week, the following timetable, recommended by the Education Authority, was implemented.

Opening 9.30 am
Morning Intervals 10.45 to 11 am and 12 to 12.05 pm
Lunch Interval   1 to 2 pm
Afternoon interval 3 to 3.05 pm
Closing 4 pm

Around this time the Public Hall went into use twice a week for Drill. It had previously been used weekly and in the early 1950s classes were held there fortnightly.

In November there was a water crisis. The supply became inadequate, a legacy of the 1955 drought from which the well had not recovered. The School Meals Department had to be informed along with the County Architect.

In 1957, for the first time, there was no annual Communion holiday in February and about this time the closures for Church-related events – Communion and Harvest Thanksgiving – were stopped and Monday holidays were given instead. This may explain why the May holiday was extended – 16th to 21st May.

At the Festival in May Tore was second out of eight choirs in their group.

The annual prizegiving, which had been in abeyance for several years, was reintroduced by Mr Mackenzie. It was an important occasion chaired by one of the local ministers while Mrs Oag, Tore Mains, WRI President, presented the prizes. Killearnan Free Church donated a Bible Prize.

The Soviet Union was leading the space race and in 1957 they put a dog into space.

1957 - 1960

When the school reopened for Session **1957 - 58** Mr Bolster, Church of Scotland minister, began visiting fortnightly to talk to the children. He had begun his ministry in Killearnan in 1956.

In September 1957 the older children were taken into the Schoolhouse to watch the first ever television broadcast to schools (a programme about British Columbia). Television (black and white) came to this part of the world in the mid-1950s with the opening of the Rosemarkie transmitter. There was one channel – BBC. Coincidentally, it was in the schoolhouse that the writer first watched TV. The Mackenzie family was one of the first to acquire a set.

One of the most newsworthy events of 1958 was a plane crash in Munich in February which almost wiped out the Manchester United football team. They were on their way home from Yugoslavia where they had played a European Cup semi-final against Red Star Belgrade. Through News reports on Television the tragedy was highlighted for a large number of people all over the country.

In June the school well dried up again. The school meals service brought water which was poured into the well and the Forestry Commission pumped five hundred gallons into a rainwater tank for the lavatories.

At the beginning of the session **1958 - 59** a boiler-house was built and a new oil-fired heating system installed. This marked the end of the old solid fuel furnace in the east room (the dining-room). It had been inefficient and also unhygienic in an area where children were eating their lunch. The redundant coal bunker was turned into a book store.

The well was again reported as giving trouble and water was carted from Munlochy. A few weeks later the village, including the school, was connected to the new Black Isle water scheme.

The road to Dingwall from the village
The roundabout is now situated a few
metres from where this photo was taken

In early January 1959 there were blizzards and the threat of blocked roads. This may have been the time referred to by Mairi Strachan when her father transported the children home. The *Ross-shire Journal* of 16th January reported that *'fall after fall of snow had accumulated to an average depth of eighteen inches. In places exposed to wind drifts were many feet deep.'*

A severe outbreak of flu in early March had serious implications for those who were to sit the Promotion Exam later in the month.

The Music Festival, in Dingwall, was also held in March. Tore school choir was placed second equal with Killen School out of nine in their class.

After the Easter break eleven infants were enrolled. This was a large class and the numbers in the school meant additional transport was required but a plea to the Authority for an extra part-time teacher fell on deaf ears.

During the session cases of ringworm and impetigo were reported. These were common problems and children were excluded from school to prevent the spread of infection. They are rarely heard of today. In the Spring an epidemic of measles reduced the attendance by over thirty pupils.

The Prizes at the annual prizegiving were presented by Mrs Bolster, Church of Scotland Manse. That year Killearnan WRI provided prizes for needlework and handwork.

In the autumn term of **1959 - 60** the Headmaster and senior boys started digging a sandpit in the playground. Around the school there were repairs to be attended to – the gate, the fence, the girls' lavatories, drainage in the playground.

Postcodes began to be used in UK in October 1959. It was also the year for a new concept in cars – the Mini which could be bought for £497.

In January 1960 heavy falls of snow with drifting caused disruption to traffic and children could not reach the school. The taxi was not able to get through nor could the meals be delivered.

All schools were granted a holiday on 22nd February to celebrate the birth of a child to the Queen. Prince Andrew, now Duke of York, was born on 19th February, the first baby born to a reigning monarch for over one hundred years.

A school concert was held shortly before the Easter holidays and raised £15 for the School Fund. Forty years ago that was a good sum of money. For £1 it was possible to buy up to eight paperback books.

After Easter ten infants were admitted taking the school roll up to sixty-four. This time a part-time teacher was appointed – Mrs Bunty MacFarquhar. She had been regularly called on to do supply and at that time two of her daughters were pupils in the school.

A royal wedding was a reason for another school holiday. On 6th May HRH Princess Margaret, sister of the Queen, married the Earl of Snowdon. It was the first British royal wedding to be widely watched on Television.

The railway line from Muir-of-Ord to Fortrose closed on 13th June 1960, having operated only for goods for the previous nine years. The local Station was sold and for most of the past forty years has operated as a coalyard.

Photograph by J.L. Stevenson

The last journey on the Black Isle line – a special passenger excursion
on 14th June 1960
The train is here stopped at Redcastle Station

11. The Sixties

This was a decade of change economically and socially. It is sometimes referred to as the 'Permissive Age' as moral standards became less strict. It is famous (or infamous) for the rise of the hippie movement in America, increasing use of drugs and music inspired by the effect of certain of these. The Vietnam war was into its second decade. The divorce rate was rising and abortion was legalised in Britain.

Audiocassettes were introduced for home use in the 1960s eventually leading to the demise of records.

Britain was applying for membership of the European Common Market but in January 1963 was denied entry. Charles De Gaulle, President of France, was blamed.

It was a decade of firsts. In 1961 the Soviet Union was the first country to send a manned satellite into space. Yuri Gagarin orbited the earth in under two hours. In 1963 the same country sent the first woman into space.

Mrs Indhira Ghandi became India's first woman Prime Minister in 1966 and in 1969 Golda Meir became the first woman to hold similar office in Israel. In 1968 the world's first heart transplant operation was performed by Dr Christian Barnard in South Africa. American astronaut Neil Armstrong was, on 20th July 1969, the first person to walk on the moon.

Pupil Memories

From the early 1960s have come many tales. Some were of canteen and carrots. The teachers sat at a separate table while keeping an eagle eye on what was happening at the other tables. Children used to hide the unwanted vegetables – especially carrots – under their leftover potato to go in the bin. The teacher knowingly would lift the potato and find them, sending the embarrassed child back to finish the food. One pupil, wise to this, smuggled out the carrots in her hankie and hid them in the sandpit. Liver, which they hated, was usually followed by a favourite pudding. No liver, no pudding. Pink custard made a lasting impression.

Another remembers reading *Treasure Island* – round the class. *'I worried so much about my turn that I had no idea what the story was about.'* This was probably true of many children who disliked reading aloud. Some tried to read ahead to 'prepare' their bit – and then lost the place. The same girl admitted, *'I was terrified of Santa at the Christmas party. It was only Donald Patience the Gym teacher.'*

Sheila MacFarquhar, who went on to become a teacher of Mathematics, spoke about *Holmes Comprehensive Arithmetic* and the hundreds (well it seemed like it) of examples on each page. It was still engendering competition and children were known to take the book home with them to do a few examples to get ahead. Some pupils hated that book so much that it put them off Maths for life.

1960

Photograph:Scholastic Souvenir Co.

Back Row: Roddy MacMillan, Billy MacKenzie, Charlie MacPhee, Ewen Cameron, Colin MacDuff- Duncan, Willie Haig, John Rose, Ian Henderson, Willie-John MacPhee, Kenneth MacKenzie, John Tolmie.
2nd Row: Lena Wilson, Alexis MacDonald, Evelyn Lochrie, Jean Wilson, Marilyn MacPhee, Fraser Gordon, Werner Schroeder, Hamish Fraser, Jimmy MacKay, Agnes Tolmie, Valerie Cameron.
3rd Row: Charlie MacPhee, Rosie MacDonald, Patricia Smith, Betty MacIntosh, Anne Gordon, Violet MacKay, Bice Percival, Virginia Fraser, Aline Oag, Janice MacRae, Christine Wilson.
4th Row: Margaret Wilson, Marlene Henderson, Joan Coburn, Anne MacIntosh, Maureen Paul, Sheila MacFarquhar, Anne MacKenzie, Catherine Tait, Maitland Jack, George Jack, Gary Cameron, Donald MacRae, Alan Henderson, Angus Campbell, Keith Dalgetty, ? MacPhee.
Front Row: Patsy MacKenzie, Sandra MacKenzie, Joan MacKenzie, Ann Duff, Maureen Duff, Mairi Mackenzie, Marilyn MacPhee, Maureen MacLeod, Iona MacDonald, Sandra Paul, Ruth MacFarquhar, Pamela Dalgetty, Patricia Dalgetty.

Mrs Gray, the Music teacher, made weekly visits. One pupil does not remember much about learning songs which they would have liked but a lot about work from the Modulator which they did not like. As the teacher pointed to the notes they had to sing them. Music lessons were held in the infant room where the piano was located and where the whole school gathered for the morning hymn and prayer. The arrival of percussion instruments changed the sound of school music. In time the canteen became more like a music room, housing the piano and other musical instruments – tambourines, tin whistles, recorders, glockenspiels and xylophones.

Staff Perspective

Although educational methods were beginning to change, much of life at school followed the old familiar patterns. Problems with the playground were ongoing and in November 1960 tarmac was laid at the back of the school. It was hoped that this would help dry out the area. Over a year later the front playground was tarred. The school roof underwent repairs where leaks had been causing damage.

On occasions over the winter there were heavy snowfalls with consequent absences and attendance was affected by the usual epidemics of mumps and chickenpox.

Among the many problems the teachers had to contend with were the results of severe frost. The children's lavatories, still housed in a separate building, froze. We recall that this had been a problem in the early days of the flush toilets but then seemed to be resolved for a time.

The annual visits by the school dentist continued as did the frequent attendance of the District Nurse to make an inspection of the children. The school doctor also carried out medical examinations of children at certain stages.

During this decade several sets of twins went through the school. Mr Mackenzie mentioned three of them. Others, younger, were Ann and Maureen Duff, Fiona and Kenneth MacKenzie and Charlie and Margaret MacPhee.

1960 - 61

Miss Jean Ainslie began work in Tore School as sewing teacher in 1960. Her visits were timetabled for Monday afternoons.

December 1960 saw the last call-up papers for National Service. Fifteen years had passed since the end of World War II and demands on the forces were decreasing.

Miss Cadger received the Infant Mistress' endorsement on her teaching certificate in May 1961 after completing several courses at Dundee College of Education during her summer holidays.

At the end of that month Rev G. Jenkins, Chairman of the Education Authority, died. He was Minister in Cromarty.

The choir which competed at the 1961 festival was unplaced but choirs from Mrs Gray's other schools took the top three

Back: Rev R. Bolster, Mrs Gray.
Front: Miss Cadger, Mr MacKenzie, Mrs MacFarquhar.

places which was gratifying for her if disappointing for the Tore pupils.

At the end of June Primary 5, 6 and 7 competed at the East-Ross Inter-school Sports in Invergordon.

1961 - 62

The Berlin Wall was constructed in August 1961 by the Communist government of East Germany to stop citizens crossing to West Germany.

In September 1961 MOT tests were introduced in this country for cars over three years old.

The District Primary Inter-school Sports were held on 7th June at Fortrose. A week later the County Music Festival took place also in Fortrose. Percussion bands from Tore competed and the Junior band (children under eight) was placed second. In solo verse-speaking (children of seven and eight) Ruth MacFarquhar was first equal with David MacLean of Killen. One of the poems was Walter De La Mare's *The Stranger*. Ruth says she came first only because she was so scared by the experience of performing that she unwittingly portrayed the atmosphere of the poem.

Little did she know that her rival would become a professional debater as MP for Penrith and the Border. After holding several ministerial offices in a Conservative Government he is at present Opposition Chief Whip in the House of Commons. Ruth herself became a teacher – involving her in public speaking although she hastened to point out that speaking to children is not exactly 'public speaking'.

In the same month Isabel MacIver, who was about to graduate BSc from Edinburgh University, spent one week's teacher training in the school. In August 1963 Miss MacIver began her career as a teacher of Mathematics in Dingwall Academy and in later years taught in Fortrose Academy. She was a former pupil of Arpafeelie and Drumsmittal Primary Schools.

At the end of the month the pupils were taken for a walk over the moor (The Moss) which lies to the north of the school. There they visited a nesting colony of black-headed gulls. The day finished with a treat of ice-cream, lemonade and biscuits. This was to become a regular excursion in the 1960s. On one occasion their expedition coincided with the RAC Scottish Rally being held in that area. The children loved it but the teachers were aware of the dangers created by flying stones and dust. An earlier generation used to frequent The Moss in search of gulls' eggs which were considered suitable for food. The direct route passes to the west of the school and was part of a road built in the 18th century by General Wade. It continues past Muckernich and on to Alcaig from where a Ferry took passengers to Dingwall. The line of this road can still be identified in The Moss.

The prizegiving took place just before the school closed for the summer holidays with Mrs MacIver, Kilcoy, President of the WRI, presenting the prizes.

1962 - 63

During the early 1960s there were several changes of Gym teacher (or PE as it came to be known). At the beginning of session 1962-63 Miss Macleman joined the staff as visiting teacher of PE in place of Mr Jock Watt. At a later date came Mrs Cattanach who was followed by Mrs Anderson in Autumn 1963. In addition to taking Gym classes in the Hall they were responsible for training athletes for the District Sports which were held in Fortrose and for the County Sports in Dingwall.

1963

Back Row: Mr A.U. Mackenzie, Keith Dalgetty, Robert Carruthers, Bobby Jack, Maitland Jack, Willie John MacPhee, Kenneth MacKenzie, Hugh Mulvey(?), Ewan Cameron, Ross MacDuff-Duncan, Charlie MacPhee, George Jack, Miss R.Cadger.
2nd Row: Alan Henderson, Joan MacKenzie, Marlene Henderson, Christine Wilson, Catherine Tait, Lena Wilson, Jean Wilson, Veronica Jack, Maureen Paul, Sheila MacFarquhar, Marilyn MacPhee, Ann MacKenzie, Ian Henderson.
3rd Row: John Dalgetty, Donald MacKenzie, Rowena Lee, Wendy Jack, Wendy Cameron, Deborah Lee, Sandra MacKenzie, Naomi MacDonald, Roslyn MacPhee, RenaMacPhee, Pamela Dalgetty, Patricia Dalgetty, Mary MacKenzie.
Front Row: Angus Chisholm, Jimmy Carruthers, George MacPhee, Patsy MacKenzie, Ruth MacFarquhar, Maureen MacLeod, Mairi Mackenzie, Joan Coburn, Sandra Paul, Gary Cameron, Billy MacKenzie.

The Beatles released their first album in 1962 and Beatlemania swept Britain and America. One lunchtime a group of girls combed their hair down in Beatles fashion and stood in wait for Miss Cadger to arrive back, expecting a remark of disapproval. They were speechless when she walked past without comment. (Did Miss Cadger know what the Beatles looked like?)

Visits to the school by policemen showing Road Safety films to the pupils were indication of economic changes which were giving rise to an increasing number of vehicles on the roads.

1963 - 64

During August and September 1963 the writer spent three weeks on teaching practice in the school. There was opportunity to spend time in both classrooms and to sit in on Music, Sewing and PE lessons with visiting teachers. Mr Mackenzie entrusted the student with individual classes which she took in the canteen. The children were well behaved and there was a pleasant atmosphere in the school.

During that term two pupils contracted scarlet fever. The other children from the same families were excluded from school for a week.

Change of leadership

Mr A. U. Mackenzie left Tore on 8th November 1963 and took up an appointment in Munlochy. Miss Cadger acted as Headteacher until a successor was appointed and Mrs Janet MacDonald from Conon-Bridge was appointed to teach the senior classes in the interim.

That same month John F. Kennedy, President of the USA, was assassinated in Dallas, Texas.

When the school opened after the Christmas holidays Mr Iain Macdonald, MA, took up duty as Headmaster.

Visits by an educational psychologist to test children were being introduced at that time and later in January 1964 a remedial teacher, Mrs Joey MacRae, was appointed to help pupils who had difficulties. Her allocation to Tore was less than two hours each day but with over fifty children in the school all help must have been welcomed.

There were changes in the nature of the promotion exams with the children being presented in a new Moray House Attainments Test in Arithmetic and in English. These tests replaced the Intelligence Tests and the Qualifying Examination and the custom of outside invigilators stopped.

At the end of June pupils competed in the District Sports and the relay team succeeded in going through to the final in Dingwall.

Just before the summer holidays the Queen and Duke of Edinburgh were in the North. They passed through the village on their way to Allangrange House before crossing on the Ferry to Inverness. The children were bussed to Kessock where they lined up on the pier. The story is told of one boy who had not gone to school that day and was among a crowd waiting at the junction at Tore to see the royal visitors pass. He was asked why people were waiting there. His response: 'I don't know.'

Parents were invited to the prizegiving and display of work on 3rd July, the day on which the school closed for the summer holidays. Mr Murray (Free Church Manse) addressed the company and Mrs Murray presented the prizes.

In 1964 many railway lines, especially in Scotland, closed – 'axed' by Dr Thomas Beeching. In June of the same year a man called Nelson Mandela was sentenced to life imprisonment in South Africa for treason. Thirty years later, in April 1994, he was elected President of South Africa. In 1993 he and the then South African President, De Klerk, had been awarded the Nobel Prize for their efforts to end apartheid.

1964 - 65

Back row: Miss Cadger, Willie John MacPhee, Maitland Jack, Lena Wilson, Sheila MacFarquhar, Catherine Tait, Marilyn MacPhee, __ , Joan Coburn, Sandra Paul, Anne MacIntosh, Christine Wilson, Kenneth MacKenzie, Maureen Paul, Mr Macdonald,
2nd Row: Ewen Cameron, Iona MacDonald, Naomi MacDonald, Anne MacKenzie, Ruth MacFarquhar, Sandra MacKenzie, Patricia Dalgetty, Maureen MacLeod, Pamela Dalgetty , Mary MacKenzie, Heather Stewart, Roslyn MacPhee, Joan MacKenzie, Patsy MacKenzie, John Tolmie.
3rd Row: John Dalgetty, __, John MacDonald, Wendy Jack, Wendy Cameron, Isobel MacKenzie, Alison MacFarquhar, Christina MacKenzie, __, Margaret Wilson, Gwen MacIntosh, Rena MacPhee, __, __, Angus Campbell, ? MacPhee, Bobby Jack.
Front Row: Gary Cameron, Kenneth Matheson, __, GeorgeMacPhee, __, __, Keith Dalgetty, Billy MacKenzie, Donald MacKenzie, Charlie MacPhee, ? MacPhee, George Jack.

Christine Hutcheson, a former pupil of Arpafeelie and Drumsmittal Primary Schools, spent two weeks of September in the school on teacher training. She is a daughter of Margaret Ann MacLean referred to in 1921.

In October 1964 the Labour Party was voted into power at the General Election and Harold Wilson became Prime Minister. One item on the Labour Party manifesto was:

> *Labour will get rid of the segregation of children into separate schools, caused by eleven-plus selection; secondary education will be reorganised on comprehensive lines.*

By the early 1970s this happened and the *'Qualifying exam was no more'*. Winston Churchill, wartime Prime Minister, died in January 1965.

After the Easter holidays there was a large intake of Infants which pushed the roll up to sixty-five. Mrs MacInnes was appointed to teach the new class along with Primary 1. These classes were taken in the canteen. At that time there was no separate kitchen area so the room contained all the canteen equipment. Because the number of pupils remained high and the room was to double as a classroom for some time, a kitchen was included in a new extension planned for the following year.

14th June 1965 was given as a holiday to mark the 700th anniversary of Parliament (1265AD). Although that had been an English Parliament it was seen as the forerunner of future parliaments.

Towards the end of the session a team took part in the District Inter-School Sports at Fortrose and Lena Wilson qualified for trials to be held in Dingwall a few days later.

The General Teaching Council to regulate the supply and training of teachers was launched in 1965. Membership was compulsory for all practising teachers, marking the end of employment of uncertificated teachers, a custom which was widespread where shortages existed.

1965 - 66

The school session began with three teachers – Mr Macdonald, Miss Cadger and Mrs MacInnes. Over the summer the floors had

been renewed and linoleum tiles laid and the electric wiring had been replaced. Prior to this the classrooms had bare wooden floors. A few weeks into the school term a polishing and washing machine arrived for Mrs MacKinnon's use, a necessity with the new type of flooring.

A 3d bit from 1967

In September a National Savings group was started up in the school with Mrs Bolster of the Church of Scotland Manse taking charge. The group was, in fact, re-started because it had already been in operation in the 1940s and 1950s. The children bought savings stamps each week and when a minimum amount was collected they were exchanged for a certificate. If left to mature (for ten years at that time) this investment yielded good interest.

New desks arrived in November. We believe these were the first since 1941. As the school closed for the Christmas holidays demolition work began on the staff room and cloakrooms in preparation for the building of new ones. The children's cloakrooms were to include toilets, a much-welcomed change from the old 'sheds' out in the playground.

Work on the extension continued throughout the year and we can imagine the inconvenience to the running of the school. Some of the buildings were not weathertight. The children's feet were muddy because of the conditions underfoot. Two of the classrooms were decorated during the Easter holidays, in spite of this major building work going on in the adjacent corridor. Above all, the distraction to the children of having workmen around must have caused grief to the teachers.

Just after the October break Mrs MacInnes, the Infant teacher, was appointed Headmistress in Torridon Primary School. The roll in Tore was fifty-two which did not justify three teachers so she was not replaced.

During December a large number of children, especially Infants, were absent suffering from measles.

In February, 1967, over a year after the work had started, the new toilets and cloakrooms were put into use. All was not straightforward: there was a problem with the heating in the girls' toilets.

Mr Macdonald recorded for us an amusing episode from that time.

> *The staff also benefited from getting a new toilet. Mrs Gray(Music teacher) on her first visit after the changes was being shown around. I opened the door to the toilet and in she went. For lack of space (the door opening inwards) I had to push myself through and shut the door behind me. The door not only shut but also locked. We were trapped and it was 2 pm. The bell had just rung for the afternoon start. No Headteacher – no music teacher – the search was on. No amount of tapping or shouting attracted any attention. Poor Mrs Gray desperate to get out of the embarrassing situation suggested she would climb through the very narrow window which had she done there would have been a call for the Fire engine.*
>
> *Then with shrieks of laughter echoing around the building Miss Cadger somehow or other saved the day. Reminds me of an old song:*
>
> > *Three old maids were locked in the lavatory*
> > *And they were there from Monday till Saturday*
> > *And nobody knew they were there.*

In more recent years a visiting school nurse succeeded in locking herself in the same infamous toilet.

North Sea oil was taken ashore in March 1967 in County Durham, the beginning of what was to become a huge industry in Britain.

The weather in June was very hot. The day of the school sports the temperature was in the high 70s and had been for several days.

1967 - 68

During the holidays the outside of the school was snowcemmed but building problems were ongoing. In the Spring the tiles in the staffroom had begun to rise because of dampness and by August the corridor tiles were doing the same.

On a happier note, a Television set was installed in the school and towards the end of the session a Tape Recorder, Record Player and Transistor Radio were brought to the school by Mr Brocklebank who was Music Organiser for the County.

A noteworthy visitor to the school was Mr Brown of the Department of Agriculture who talked to the pupils about mink. He brought with him a live ferret and a mink in cages and a selection of stuffed animals which in addition to mink included a pine marten, an otter and some smaller species.

As part of the curriculum the school was using the SRA Reading Laboratory, popular and successful in the 1960s and 1970s. Children progressed through this reading scheme at their own level of ability.

1968 - 69

The school roll was low – forty-one pupils – at the beginning of this session. There were just two infants in that intake. One child from the Allanglach area had been transferred to Munlochy because of a new transportation policy.

At this time Mr Petrie was Primary School Organiser and appears to have been the first person to occupy this position.

The Royal Mail introduced first and second class postage in September 1968. First class cost 5d (just under 2½p) and second class cost 4d.

The government had decreed that British Summer Time should continue to operate throughout the winter which meant that daylight did not arrive until about 9 am. In school the usual winter timetable went into operation but instead of closing early classes started later to ensure that the children were not leaving home in darkness. The experiment was not repeated.

Back: Mrs McKinnon
Front: Miss Cadger, Mr MacDonald, Miss Ainslie

During the Christmas holidays new vinyl tiles were laid in the corridor, kitchen and staffroom but by February those in the staffroom were again rising.

In June the children in Primary 4 to 7 had their annual excursion, this year to Urquhart Castle.

The Primary 7 pupils who moved on to Secondary School in 1969 were all faced with the prospect of being at school until they were sixteen. The school leaving age was going to be raised from fifteen in 1973 and this was the first group to be affected.

The Age of Projects

1969 - 70

For the first time the school was allocated a visiting Art teacher, Mr D. Webster, who started in August 1969.

Later in the session an Inspector visited. Mr Macdonald explains the outcome of that visit.

> *I was approached by the Inspectorate to try out a project in which Art was to become an important tool in developing writing skills – stories, poems etc., these in turn giving a new impetus to the Art side. This proved to be very successful and indeed it gave the pupils a liking for both Art and Language Skills. They tackled their tasks with gusto and lovely work flowed from their pens and I still read their poems and stories with delight and wonder – beautiful jewels of thought – full of expression.*

Mr Crawford, the Art Organiser, worked at the school one day or a half day each week. The artist, Allan Macdonald, son of the Headmaster, was a young pupil in the school at the time. We have his account of the projects.

> *My lasting memory was of the big projects which seemed to take over the school each year, always with a different theme. The one that has stayed with me is 'Dreamantlis', a project based on a make-believe, mythical city beneath the sea. I still remember the school taking on a sort of shimmering green appearance as the windows were covered in blue paint and green tissue paper. I think the other thing that impacted on my young mind was the scale of everything. Many projects in schools, even today, seem quite unambitious by comparison. Whole walls were covered in huge pictures which appeared to envelop the classroom, dinosaurs stretched from the floor to the ceiling, and a general ferment of artistic activity prevailed throughout the school. Now this has to be put in context; one, against a fairly sterile creative environment in schools at the time, and two, what we see today where Art is squeezed into an overcrowded timetable and made to compete with PE amongst other things. I don't think it is just rose tinted spectacles either. The school was highly commended at the time, and it was used as an example across the North East, showing the potential of Art for developing a more rounded child. Also, the evidence remains in the outstanding poetry, better than any child's literature I've ever seen.*

Personally, I think it was a major formative experience for me, since I have ended up as a professional artist. The sheer magic of creating, the joy of colour and texture, and the ambitious scale have had a lasting impact on my work today. So thanks, Dad.

Eighteen schools – teachers and pupils – visited Tore to see the project work which was a new concept then. Mr Macdonald was pleased with the way his pupils explained to the visitors step by step the work done on their  project. Pupils from Tore also visited other schools involved in project work for interchange of ideas. A member of Her Majesty's Inspectorate for Art was very impressed by the pupils' work. The magazine, *Education in the North,* contained an article by Mr Macdonald and Mr Crawford describing the work.

Enjoying their work

Whether the project was a success or not one thing is certain, it was a rich and exciting experience for teacher and pupils alike and it would be difficult to say who had learned most.

To those of us who watched the children work it became very obvious that there was a great willingness to participate and to learn.

The Heart of the Community

Over the years the school was used by a variety of outside bodies. We have already mentioned the Church services in the early part of the century and the Sunday School begun in the fifties and continuing until 2000. In addition there were lectures and evening classes. Neil Macleod, whose father was Headmaster from 1946 to 1956, wrote:

The school rooms were used by associations the most popular of which was The Beekeepers who presented a lecture and slideshow. Audiences were small often only the Headteacher and family and sometimes just the family – our only entertainment for months!

Evening classes of the sixties included Country Dancing, Sewing, Psalmody and Leather Craft. Mrs Cooper taught the Sewing Class where the women made skirts and Miss Campbell inspired a group of ladies to produce beautiful leather handbags. Mr Colvin Greig instructed an adult class in Psalmody and, in the sixties and seventies, Rev Hugh MacKay Free Church minister took a group of children for Psalmody after school.

Back: Jacqueline MacRae.
Middle Row:Isobel MacLennan,Shona Macdonald, Heather Campbell, Catriona MacRae.
Front:__, Christine Ferguson.

Kenneth MacKenzie, Brian Dalgetty, David MacLennan, Charlie McPhee.

Children of the Seventies

Back: __, Moira Fraser.
Front: Margaret MacPhee, Mairi MacDonald Fiona MacKenzie.

12. Celebrating a Centenary

Changes in education accelerated during this decade. Secondary education became Comprehensive and the school leaving age was, about the same time, raised to sixteen. Towards the end of the decade reforms were proposed in the qualifications achieved in Secondary Schools, particularly to accommodate the academically less able pupils who previously would have chosen to leave school at fifteen.

Videocassettes became available to consumers in the early 1970s enabling teachers to record schools programmes to show at a later date – and more convenient time.

Community Councils were formed in the mid-1970s according to the Community Council Act (1973). A good relationship was established between the school and the Killearnan Community Council and a donation is still given to the school each year from the Council at Christmas time.

Mrs MacKinnon, who had been cleaner and dinner-lady since the fifties, retired early in this decade and Mrs Gwen Jack took over her duties.

1970 - 71

Page from book compiled from pieces on Enchanted Forest

Prehistoric Forests was the theme of the Language Arts programme for this session and another successful project was carried out.

1971 began with a major postal strike cutting communication by letter for several weeks. (And remember e-mail did not exist at that time.)

On 15th February the country's money system was decimalised (the system in use today). In the run-up to this change schools were preparing children for it. It altered the whole concept of 'money sums', removing an area of Arithmetic which had given much difficulty to children. (Some detail of the old system was given in Chapter 2.)

The Moray House Verbal Reasoning Tests were held for the last time. With comprehensive education replacing selection and streaming there was no more need for a promotion examination.

An innovation (and a sign that life in society was changing) was a programme of visits by the police to talk to the children. From the 1970s there were regular visits: alerting children to the dangers of drugs, of talking to strangers; and giving advice on good citizenship. In addition they continued to instruct in Road Safety and to test in cycling proficiency for which the children received a certificate.

In 1971 the choir from Tore gained second place in the two-teacher schools section. Another interesting result from that Festival was that of the speech solo in the seven to nine age group. A girl from Maryburgh School took first place. Her name – Margo MacLennan, who twenty-five years later was to become Headteacher of Tore School.

1971 - 72

The school roll continued to fall and at the start of this session was down to twenty-seven pupils. The large classes of the sixties were moving through the school and leaving for Secondary School while the number of infants being enrolled was small. There was only one new pupil in August 1971.

Project work was ongoing and the Needlework teacher became involved. The library service also gave support by providing boxes of books on the project theme. By this time Mr Wright was the Primary Schools Adviser.

The usual medical inspections and innoculations were taking place and girls were being innoculated against rubella. In the early Log Books German measles had been frequently cited as reasons for absence. It was considered a mild disease but in 1941 an Australian discovered that some congenital deformities in babies were caused by the mother contracting rubella while pregnant. In 1962 the virus was isolated and in 1969 a vaccine was made available.

Nurse MacInnes, who regularly visited the school, retired in January 1972. She had been in the area for thirty-one years and lived in a cottage (designated for the District Nurse) in Munlochy. Many of the children of the forties were 'her' babies, at a time when home deliveries by the District Nurse were the norm. Later generations, although born in hospital, were under her watchful eye as they developed and as they went to school. That lady had built up a very special relationship with mothers and children in her district.

Early in the New Year a situation arose which was to cause disruption in the country. A miners' strike lasted for seven weeks and many workplaces were put on to a three-day week to conserve electricity supplies.

1972 - 73

Iain Macdonald left Tore in 1972 to take up the post of Headmaster at Kiltearn Primary School.

He has written about his time at Tore.

> *I would say that in all my years as a teacher my time spent as*
> *Headteacher at Tore School was definitely the happiest.*
> *As far as being a Head for the first time I was as one would say*
> *in army terms a complete Rookie. However I was very fortunate*

*in that the outgoing Head, Alasdair Mackenzie, a man of wisdom
and tact proved to be a most reliable help and guide when needed.
I must also mention Miss Cadger, teacher of the early primaries
who kept me on an even keel. She had a lovely disposition,
never could be riffled and was loved by all her pupils. Her work
was thorough. It was very evident that she was totally devoted
to her career. I was pleased that on my moving on she was
elected Headteacher.*

*The pupils were a fine happy bunch of youngsters and there
were seldom any disciplinary problems. I think it helped in
those days that the school started the day with religious
instruction from Primary 1 upwards. Alas this has gone.*

*The pupils at the higher end did not have an easy time as
decimalisation took over and after learning all the intricacies of
the older and original way these had to be abandoned, and yet
for years afterwards we were still buying petrol by the gallon,
milk by the pint and sugar by the pound. A new method of
writing was also introduced to compound the existing difficulties.*

Mr Macdonald, in addition to describing his experiences as Headteacher,
has written his feelings about living in this community.

*I simply loved living in those pleasant surroundings and many
a morning I was up very early walking or cycling enjoying the
fresh air and the scenery, the peace and quiet at that time of
day. If I happened to pass Dunleary, home of the MacFarquhar
family, I was always kindly invited in for a ' cuppa hot tea'.
Greatly appreciated! Mrs MacFarquhar was an early bird!
Many changes have come to Tore since those days. I well
remember the narrow twisty road down to the ferry for Inverness
– then the quicker route. It would have been but a mad dream to
have thought of the dual carriageway now running through
the village. The peaceful element has departed; the throb of
engines racing has taken over.*

By the time Mr Macdonald left, the number of pupils had fallen
to nineteen so the school was reduced to one teacher and Miss Cadger was
appointed Headteacher.

There were no classroom assistants, auxiliaries or clerical assistance in
those days. The Headteacher did everything and although the roll increased
an assistant was not appointed until the following session. After Mr
Macdonald's time the schoolhouse was not used by the Headteacher so it was
let to another teacher employed in the County.

The idea of in-service days for teachers was introduced about this time. This was the first school year to begin with a day for teachers without the pupils. It was to become the norm that, after (or sometimes before) certain holidays, the teachers would have a day for development work or to attend courses.

On 20th November 1972 schools were granted a holiday to mark the Queen and Prince Philip's Silver Wedding. Their wedding day in 1947 had also been a holiday.

Britain finally joined the Common Market in January 1973 and in April of the same year Value Added Tax (VAT) replaced purchase tax.

The mid-term holiday was taken on the 7th of May to comply with a government ruling that the first Monday in May be a Bank Holiday. The trade unions had been pushing for years for 1st May to be a public holiday as it was in many other countries.

The Rector of Fortrose Academy visited the school in June in connection with the transfer of Primary 7 pupils. A few days later the four pupils in that class spent an introductory day in the Academy. That was a successful experiment and within three years was extended to a whole week.

In early June all the pupils attended the Festival with a small choir taking part. The Music teacher at this time was Mrs West who visited the school weekly. At the end-of-year prizegiving the prizes were presented by Mrs MacKay whose husband, Hugh, was minister of Killearnan Free Church and who made regular visits to the school to take assemblies.

1973 - 74

This session began with two in-service days for the teachers before the pupils arrived back. Miss Noble, who had been appointed as Assistant Teacher when the roll increased, found herself in charge because Miss Cadger had leave of absence due to family illness. The roll was twenty-two. Four pupils had gone to Fortrose Academy and four infants were enrolled. To begin with Mrs MacLeman was temporary assistant and later Mrs MacKenzie took over and remained until Miss Cadger returned. Mr Dunn started work in the school as Art teacher.

Early in the session Mr Hayes of the Leprosy Mission visited the school and talked about work being done to help people suffering from leprosy. A few weeks later the writer was invited to show slides of the work of a school in Lima, Peru, where she had been teaching.

A holiday was granted to the children in honour of the marriage of Princess Anne and Captain Mark Phillips on 14th November. Many people bought their first colour TV set at this time.

A severe snowstorm in December caused many schools in the area to close for the two days prior to the Christmas holidays. In Tore the Christmas party was postponed and took place early in January. The schools opened very soon after New Year – on 3rd January.

In June Rev Hugh Mackay, attending the school to take an assembly, was accompanied by Rev Prakash Kumar, an Indian pastor, who addressed the children. He then visited them in their classrooms.

1974 - 75

After the summer holidays three children went to Fortrose Academy and one to Dingwall Academy. Because Miss Cadger was absent Miss Noble was again in charge of the school.

Miss Ogilvie, the new Primary Adviser, visited the school early in the session as did PE and Home Economics Advisers, the Educational Psychologist and the Assistant Director of Education, Allan Gilchrist.

Since the Headteacher no longer occupied the schoolhouse a telephone extension from the schoolhouse was installed in the school in January 1975.

About this time a course of swimming lessons was given to the children of Primary 5, 6 and 7 at Dingwall Sports Centre. This was to become an annual feature of the timetable and later included the younger children also.

In May and June the police carried out an eight-week cycling proficiency course (one day each week). At the end of this six pupils were tested.

Miss Noble was very interested in Verse-speaking and for the Festival in June she trained and presented pupils from Primary 2,3 and 4 in Solo Speech. One pupil gained first place, three

Back:David MacLennan, Fiona MacRae
Front: Alan Tolmie, Marion MacKenzie, Yvonne MacPhee, Francis MacLeod

gained second place and four gained third place. She also had a group take part in an action piece.

At the prizegiving in Tore Hall Rev Hugh MacKay chaired the proceedings and Mrs Bolster presented the prizes. Following the event the school was open for parents to see an exhibition of work.

A major change in local government took place in 1975. Groups of County Councils were amalgamated into larger administrative regions. The counties of Caithness, Sutherland, Ross & Cromarty (except Lewis), Inverness (except Harris and the outer isles), Nairn and a small part of Moray became Highland Regional Council with its offices in Inverness. The islands mentioned formed the Western Isles Council. Schools became the responsibility of Highland Regional Council but in the Districts – Ross and Cromarty was one – a Divisional Education Officer (now Area Education Manager) directed the local scene.

1975 - 1979

The school roll was rising again and at the beginning of **1975 -76** there were twenty-eight pupils.

The annual course of swimming lessons started on 14th January 1976 with six pupils from Primary 5-7 at Dingwall Sports Centre.

That same month Concorde took off simultaneously from London and Paris. Less than thirty years later that exceptional plane was to be taken out of service and became a museum piece.

In June the Primary 7 pupils spent a whole week in Fortrose on an induction course. It was such a successful venture that it became an annual practice. Around the same time an epidemic of measles struck the younger children and attendance was down to less than half.

January of **1977** was stormy and on the 14th the pupils were sent home after lunch because of a snowstorm.

Shortly before the school closed for Easter that year Mr Cooper from Moray House College of Education visited in connection with a Geography 10 - 14 project for Primary and Secondary Schools.

In May Miss Ogilvie, the Primary Adviser, took Primary 6 and 7 pupils to see the work on the Cromarty Bridge being built on the north side of the Black Isle as part of the new A9 road. The Bridge was to become an important link between the Black Isle and Easter Ross.

The Queen's Silver Jubilee was celebrated in 1977 and schools were closed on 6th June to mark the occasion. A group of parents and other local people arranged a sports day for the community. A large number turned out for this event which took place at the football pitch – at that time the field to the west of the school. Teas were served in the Public Hall. The souvenir mugs in which the tea was served were offered for sale afterwards. All the children received a gift of a Silver Jubilee bank.

JubileeBank

In August 1977 Elvis Presley, the rock legend, died. His music is still popular and fans continue to visit his home in Memphis in the United States.

Early in **1978** the weather was stormy. On the last weekend of January a blizzard raged over Northern Scotland, blocking roads, bringing down electricity lines and telephone wires. The school was closed from 30th January until 9th February because of the snow and prolonged lack of power. There was a further snowstorm a week later and the school closed again over two days, followed a few days later by another closure when a new burner had to be fitted to the boiler. The oil had frozen during severe frost.

During this time discussions began which were to radically change the examination system in Secondary Schools, leading to the introduction of Standard Grades and the phasing out of O-Grades.

In **1979** the school opened on 4th January but because of falling snow and consequent dangerous road conditions the children were sent home.

A General Election took place on 3rd May 1979 and the school was used as the polling station for residents of the Parish of Killearnan. The Conservatives gained power and Margaret Thatcher became Britain's first woman Prime Minister. Elections for the European Assembly took place on 7th June and again the school was used. Killearnan School had traditionally been the polling station until it closed. More recently the use of schools was discontinued and in the Parish of Killearnan voters now go to Tore Hall.

Later in June nine pupils took part in a rounders tournament held at Ferintosh School. The school outing in the summer term was a drive on the new road from Tore to Findon, across the Cromarty Bridge and back. They then drove to Cromarty where time was spent on the beach. The children had a picnic lunch in Cromarty School.

At the end of June Miss Noble retired. She presented the prizes at the prizegiving and the staff and children presented her with an electric fire and a bouquet of flowers. On the day prior to the school closing Alan Forsyth, Divisional Education Officer, Miss Ogilvie and Miss Laing visited the school to see Miss Noble.

Centenary Year 1979 - 80

When the school resumed in August Miss Dorothy-Anne Morrison joined the staff from Strathconon School. She belonged to Ballinluig in Perthshire.

A week after the session began a colour TV was installed and, almost like a step back in time, a Transistor Radio was delivered in December.

On 27th October the school celebrated its Centenary. The teachers created an exhibition of Victorian artefacts and photographs. The *People's Journal* ran an article with the accompanying photograph. Part of that article is reproduced (with permission) below.

> *To mark the centenary the teachers have been discussing what life, both in and out of school, would have been like a century ago.*
>
> *For a couple of afternoons each week, Miss Morrison has been changing her classroom back to what it might have looked like back in 1879, with an open-fire poster on the wall and all modern gadgets removed.*
>
> *The children have been experimenting with writing on slates similar to those their great-grandparents would have used.*

At the end of January 1980 a frost protection device and thermostat were installed which meant that when the temperature fell to a certain point the heating came on.

The teachers spent the 12th May at an in-service course on Primary School Mathematics delivered by lecturers from Aberdeen College of Education. Three days later the same lecturers visited the school.

In June four pupils took part in a swimming gala in Dingwall. Fiona MacRae won the girl's race from Group D. The school outing took place later in the month and the venue was Cawdor Castle. Remember that outings, a hundred years ago, were to the neighbouring parish and in 1894 the children were taken as far as Fortrose!

The President of the WRI, Mrs Dalgetty, presented the prizes at the prizegiving. Every child received an award. In addition to providing money for prizes in Needlework and Handwork, the WRI gave a donation for outings and parties.

Photograph taken to mark the Centenary

Photograph: D.C. Thomson Ltd

Back Row: Jackie Grant, Iain MacRae, Alan Fraser, Alan Tolmie, Steven Ross, Douglas Jack, Leslie Steven, Garry Bain, Graham MacLennan.
2nd Row Miss Dorothy Morrison, Fiona MacRae, Marion MacKenzie, Norma MacKay, Michael Fraser, Miss Rena Cadger, Tracy Grant.
3rd Row: Alison Matheson, Elaine Macrae, Jayne Henderson, Andrea Dalgetty, Alison Fraser, Lorraine Steven, Wendy Jack, Heather MacLeod, Donald Fraser.
Front Row: Donald MacRae, Steven MacKay, Lauren Soutar, Alistair MacLennan, Morag MacLeod, Murdo Matheson, Alistair Jack.

Around this time Mr Norman Macleod, former Headteacher, called at the school. Mr Macleod still enjoyed his riddles. He asked the children a 'difficult' question: *'On which side of the cup is the handle?'* The obvious answers were offered such as 'the right', 'the left'. It took some headscratching before one boy put up his hand and tentatively offered 'the outside?' He was rewarded with a 50p piece.

Children of the eighties on a field trip

13. A Decade of Change

This decade saw further changes in education. One major innovation was the setting up of School Boards in 1989 fulfilling the provision of the 1988 School Boards Act (Scotland). These were different from the School Boards which had been responsible for running the 19th Century schools.

The new Boards were groups of elected parents and staff and co-opted non-parent members from the local community. They were given power to discuss and approve aspects of school policy and school development planning, and to be involved in staff appointments at senior level.

Another change was the publication of the Parents' Charter of 1988 giving parents freedom of choice of school for their children. It took time for this to have much impact in the case of Tore School but recent years have shown a marked increase in the number of placing requests from parents outwith the traditional catchment area.

On the world scene there was, as always, good news and bad. In 1980 the World Health Organisation declared the eradication of smallpox – three years had passed without one reported case of the disease. Because of vaccination it had been almost unheard of in the 20th Century in Scotland. Tragically, in 1981 Centres for Disease Control reported a new disease which has gone on to kill thousands of people worldwide – AIDS.

Compact Discs began to appear in record stores and within ten years had all but replaced vinyl records and were beginning to overtake cassettes.

In 1981 the United States began its space shuttle programme, for the first time sending a reusable spacecraft to make the return journey to earth.

1980 - 81

The school year began for the pupils on 20th August. Heating engineers installed a new boiler in September.

In the midde of November work began to prepare a site for six Council houses opposite the school. That meant, for the school, loss of the stunning view from the windows. Generations of children had drawn, painted and written about that view of farmland and woodland with a backdrop of distant mountains. Children were made aware of the changing seasons: spring when the trees burst into leaf and the farmers prepared the fields for crops; summer as the crops grew and the wild roses bloomed and the sunshine tantalised those 'imprisoned' observers; autumn with the leaves turning various shades of red and brown and the farmers reaping the ripened corn; winter drew little eyes toward the hills, looking for the first snows – the promise of unexpected days off as the season deepened.

Two days after the work began on the houses there was a heavy snowfall – several inches by lunchtime. Transport was ordered and the pupils were sent home – certainly unexpected in November.

After the Christmas break Miss Morrison was unable to reach school on the first morning because of a snowstorm during the weekend. For over a week there were problems. Because of the wintry conditions the minibus was unable to collect children.

The existence of the minibus highlights a new development. With the building of the new A9 routed across the Black Isle a traffic danger emerged. Since plans did not include a footbridge or underpass over this busy road the Council provided transport for all children whose journey to school took them across the road. Jessie Cumming, the minibus driver, is now transporting the second generation of Tore children to and from school.

Miss Cadger attended a Religious Education seminar in Inverness in March 1981. By this time the Region had an Adviser in RE who organised such events. The subject had changed over the previous decade and the syllabus with much memory work had been discarded.

In June there was a school outing to Inverness where the pupils visited the fire station and police Headquarters.

1981 - 82

By November 1981 some of the houses opposite the school were occupied and families which moved in there were to contribute to the school roll for several years to come.

About this time a separate telephone was installed in the school to replace the extension from the schoolhouse phone. Fortunately the system of party lines had been discontinued several years earlier.

In-service days for teachers were becoming regular occurrences and in November the school closed for a Language Arts in-service course at Cullicudden School.

A few days later Garry Bain, a pupil in Primary 7, fell while playing football at lunchtime and broke his leg. He spent some days in Raigmore Hospital. (That was before the present hospital was constructed.) Garry had his leg in plaster until after Christmas.

In late November Mr Mein, HMI, made a general inspection. Within two years HMI reports would be published.

The winter of 1981- 82 was severe, causing disruption in school. Early in December the heating system broke down when, during hard frost, the oil supply froze so the children were sent home. A few days later a heavy fall of snow meant another early closure with a repeat on the following day when, because the oil had frozen again, there was no heating.

Ross-shire schools were due to reopen on 6th January 1982 after the Christmas holidays but because of snowstorms in the preceding three days they remained closed. There then occurred a series of events which must have inconvenienced the staff but probably delighted the children since it meant extra holidays. The roads remained hazardous and the heating failed.

The Queen's visit
Kessock Ferry, June 1964

A sixties group dressed for an outing

A Page from
The Enchanted Forest
- a Project of the 1970s

(The oil pipe was again frozen). Then a pipe in the canteen burst. Because there was severe frost the heating was switched on over the weekend but on Monday there was a power cut so it was 12th January before the pupils returned to school. But there was another complication – because Munlochy School had no water supply (frozen pipes) no school meals were provided.

The following day the children were sent home early following a call from the Education Centre warning that roads were becoming blocked by lying snow drifting in a strong wind. The school remained closed on the 14th because of the road conditions. Routes to Dingwall and the Cromarty Bridge were closed at the roundabout. It was the 19th of January before school meals were again being supplied.

In March a meeting was held as a follow-up from the in-service day in November on Language Arts. This meeting was held in Tore so the pupils went home after lunch.

Britain went to war with Argentina in April over the Falkland Islands, British territory which Argentine troops had invaded. The war lasted seventy-four days and ended in victory for British troops.

On 4th May the Prince of Wales was paying a visit to the Abbeyfield House in Rosemarkie and the pupils were bussed there to see him. In June the school outing took place to Kincraig Wildlife Park.

Children (and adults) in 1982 delighted in the film E.T. about a loveable alien.

1982 - 83

During the summer holidays the Kessock Bridge was opened, Queen Elizabeth the Queen Mother performing the ceremony. This Bridge meant the end of the Kessock Ferry but it also meant that the new A9 became extremely busy since motorists from the North and West, heading for Inverness and further, availed themselves of this shorter and faster route.

Early in the term a photocopier was delivered to the school. To a generation which takes this machine for granted it may seem like an insignificant event but in 1982 photocopying was a very new concept. Prior to that there were ink printers, sometimes known as Gestetners, for which stencils had to be cut using a typewriter without its ribbon. The printing could be a messy task. There were also Banda machines which used carbon stencils – typed or handwritten. Paper dampened with special fluid picked up the carbon and about a hundred copies could be made. The photocopier was to be a major asset to the classroom teacher and one which is now indispensable.

An in-service day in October took place at Bridgend School, Alness, where Mr A.U. Mackenzie formerly of Tore and then Munlochy was Headmaster. The theme of the day was Environmental Studies – an area which had been introduced into the curriculum to embrace subjects such as Science, History, Geography and others.

The following month Mr Douglas Willis, Principal Teacher of Geography in Fortrose Academy, visited on two occasions and gave the older classes a lesson on local geography. Other visitors that term were Billy and Elizabeth Graham who spoke about their work in South Africa where Mr Graham was Principal of a Theological College. They showed slides and let the children hear a tape of African singing. Interestingly, Mrs Wilson, Headteacher in 2004, and her family have moved to South Africa where her husband has taken up an appointment in that same College.

The early months of 1983 were less stormy than in some of the previous years with few unexpected closures. Snow at the end of the month resulted in the children being sent home and in early February the school was closed because of an interruption to the electricity supply.

Primary 7 pupils were taken in April to Tarradale Primary School to hear a talk on the history of making lutes. Some of the instruments were played and a soprano sang a selection of Elizabethan and other music.

A team of girls competed in a netball tournament held in May in the Sports Centre in Dingwall.

In May the Scottish Education Department announced that from session 1983 - 84 HMI reports on schools were to be published. They became available for all who were interested and summaries appeared in the newspapers – not, unfortunately, always highlighting the good points of a school.

Two pupils who took part in a swimmimg gala, in Alness in June, both gained first place. One of those was Douglas Hiddleston who set a new record.

On 9th June a General Election took place and the school was used as a polling station. Margaret Thatcher led the Conservatives into power for a second term of office. In Ross & Cromarty Charles Kennedy, Liberal Democrat, defeated Hamish Gray who had been Conservative MP since 1970. Kennedy was the youngest Member of Parliament when he took his seat.

The annual outing took place to Brodie Castle and Culloden and on 22nd June eight pupils took part in Inter-School Sports.

As usual a prizegiving was held at the end of the session. The two local ministers, Rev Richard Bolster of the Church of Scotland and Rev Hector Cameron of the Free Church, took part and Mrs Cameron presented the prizes. Throughout this session the local ministers had been involved in leading the Assemblies.

It is difficult to imagine life without e-mail but it was only in 1983 that the internet was established, e-mail being one of its uses. It would be at least ten years before it came into widespread use.

1983 - 84

In the early days of the session visitors to the school included two ladies from Britoil who gave an illustrated talk on the Beatrice Field, sited off the coast of Caithness. A few days later there was the annual medical inspection of certain age-groups. Dr Jackson was at that time Schools Medical Officer. Mr Tom Adair, newly-appointed Adviser for Primary Schools, called early in September.

A BBC microcomputer was obtained this term. It was one of the forerunners of the Personal Computer and was mainly used for operating educational programmes. These were initially accessed from tapes but within two years disk drives became available which used 5-inch (12.5cm) floppy disks. A couple of months after the arrival of the computer, teachers attended an in-service course on its use.

A Video Cassette Recorder was delivered to the school in January 1984. Technology had come a long way since the delivery of the black and white television set in 1967.

January and February 1984 were particularly difficult months weatherwise. There were several storms, with drifting snow creating problems on the roads, and severe frost caused the heating oil to freeze. As was fairly usual for this time of year there were early closures and days of extra holiday for the pupils.

The range of sports available to the children was increasing and in March the senior pupils took part in badminton matches in Conon School.

Back Row: Alison Fraser, Douglas Jack, Garry Bain, Alistair Jack, Tracey Urquhart.
2nd Row: Amy Clark, Steven MacKay, Donald Fraser, Alan Fraser, Steven Ross, Jackie Grant, Alison Matheson, Jane Macpherson, Lorna Grant, Mandy Jack.
3rd Row: Miss Dorothy Morrison, Ewen Fraser, Alistair MacLennan, Graham MacKay, Bobby Jack, Murdo Matheson, Donald MacRae, Paul Henderson, David Bain, Angus Soutar, Paul Murray, Mark Haynes.
Front Row: Grace Soutar, Morag Macleod, Wendy Jack, Lorraine Steven, Elaine MacRae, Heather Macleod, Julie MacLennan, Lauren Soutar, Sonia Macdonald, Linda Jack.

Some pictures
from the
Jubilee Sports 1977

1984

TORE
PRIMARY-SCHOOL
TORE
1984

Photograph by Fotek

Back Row: David Bain, Alisdair Mackenzie, Christopher Urquhart, Douglas Hiddleston, Murdo Matheson, Paul Henderson, Thomas MacLean.
2nd Row: Miss Cadger, Wendy Jack, Elaine MacRae, Alison Fraser, Claire Cameron, Alison Matheson, Heather Macleod, Lorraine Steven, Amanda Petrie, Mrs Kinnear.
3rd Row: Scott MacPherson, Ruaraidh Ross, Mark Haynes, Alistair Raeburn, Ewen Fraser, Donald MacRae, Steven MacKay, Graham MacKay, Paul Murray, Alistair MacLennan, Gary Murray, George Jack.
FrontRow: Kerrie MacLean, Joanne MacRae, Amy Clark, Adele Cameron, Linda Jack, Sonia MacDonald, Justine McChristie, Morag MacLeod, Andrea Dalgetty, Susan Petrie, Davina MacLean.

On 30th March school closed for the Easter holidays. Dorothy-Anne Morrison, assistant teacher for the previous five years, left because she was getting married in June. Mrs Diane Kinnear was appointed temporarily in her place. Four children spent the first week of the summer term on an educational trip to London along with pupils from Conon School.

Pupils took part in a swimming gala at Alness Academy. Douglas Hiddleston won Group D boys' freestyle event and broke his own record from the previous year. Thirteen of the children took part in the Primary Inter-School sports in Dingwall and won the shield for their Group.

Landmark Centre, Carrbridge, was the venue for the annual outing with a return trip via Grantown and Nairn.

In 1984 Ted Hughes was appointed poet laureate; Desmond Tutu, a black South African, received the Nobel prize for his work against apartheid and in July the Prince of Wales married Lady Diana Spencer. Since the wedding took place during the summer holidays the children missed out on the customary Royal Wedding holiday.

At some time between 1980 and 1984 the school day was shortened by ten minutes – to close at 3.50 instead of 4 pm.

1984 - 85

P1-3 1984-85

Photograph: Andrew Allan

Back: Paul Murray, Mark Haynes, Ewan Fraser, Linda Jack, Joanne MacRae, Gary Murray, Kerry MacLean, Susan Petrie.
Front: Angus Ross, James MacDonald, Peter Haynes, Kelly MacRae, Gregor Jack, Ruaraidh Ross.

When the school resumed in August Miss Margaret Buchanan, from Dingwall Primary School, joined the staff as teacher of Primary 1 to 4.

A Baby Belling cooker was delivered to school in October. From then the children were given lessons in baking small items such as Queen cakes.

In November the pupils participated in a fund-raising event for Ethiopian Famine Relief. They gave up their playtime snack and donated the value. Some pupils brought warm clothing which was to be sent to famine victims.

The Road Safety Officer, Mrs Marjory Miller, visited the school in November and again in December when she showed slides and a video to the children.

In May 1985, along with pupils from other Black Isle schools, some of Primary 6 and 7 took part in a performance of 'The Snow Queen' at Eden Court Theatre.

Mr Macleod, rector of Fortrose Academy, called in June to talk to pupils who would be attending there the following session. Those pupils spent the following week at the Academy.

Wendy Jack competed in a swimming gala at Alness and the school was second in their group at the Inter-school Sports. Newhall School took a majority of the first places but for Tore Wendy Jack, David Bain and Morag MacLeod were all placed in events.

Dunrobin Castle was the venue for the 1985 annual school outing.

1985 - 86

The Windows operating system for computers was established in 1985.

In September the wreckage of the ocean liner, the Titanic, sunk in 1912, was discovered at a depth of four thousand metres.

At school Mrs Green of the Royal Scottish Society for the Prevention of Cruelty to Children (now known as Children 1st) visited and told the pupils about the work of the Society encouraging them to take part in sponsored fund-raising. They raised £220 in a sponsored spell.

During their dinner hour pupils (both boys and girls) knitted squares which were then made into a rug. Miss Buchanan took some of the children to Urray House to hand it over for the use of residents there. They were entertained to juice and cake.

In October a little comfort was granted to the teachers – a carpet was fitted in the staffroom.

On April 25-26, 1986, a serious accident occurred at the Chernobyl nuclear power station in the Soviet Union, the worst in the history of nuclear power generation. Radioactivity was spread by the wind over several countries and soon reached as far west as France. Millions of acres of forest and farmland were contaminated.

The school outing in June was to Kingussie Folk Museum. Rena Cadger retired at the summer holidays after thirty-six years at the school and was presented with a large number of gifts including a silver teaservice and a teaset. She recalls the large celebration cake which was made by one of the mothers – Mickey Bain. Miss Cadger holds the record for the longest serving teacher in Tore school.

In July Prince Andrew married Sarah Ferguson but since this was summer holiday time the children again missed out on the extra day's closure usually granted for a royal wedding.

Mrs Clasper

1986 - 89

When the school resumed in August 1986 Mrs Val Clasper took up duty as Headteacher. She had been Headteacher in Park school in Invergordon.

I was very very happy at Tore and remember with affection all the Christmas Concerts that Margaret Buchanan and I put on — where every single child in the school was included.

In my time the 'hall' was known as the L.J.P. room which stood for love, joy, peace. And unless you were living up to these principles (with the other children) in there you had to

leave the room and go elsewhere. Interestingly once I had explained what and why it was L.J.P. we never in seven years had to throw anyone out.

We began every day with an assembly and at Christmas had special ones where we opened the advent calendars. At these get togethers we all sat in a circle, which was known as "the circle of love" because Jesus was born in love for all of us.

We had a school band, which again involved everyone, and that was great fun; the music teacher at that time was

very gifted and inspired us all to persevere to a high standard.

I remember the snowmen we made out in the playground when all the little ones were paired with the bigger ones and worked as a team.

Back Row: Donna MacLean, Joanne MacRae, Susan Petrie, Gary Murray, Philip Balfour, Gregor Jack, Paul Murray, David Bain.
2nd Row: Ewan Fraser, Miss M. Buchanan, Mark Haynes, Kerry MacLean, Scott MacPherson, Angus Ross, Ross Fraser, Kelly MacRae, Ruaraidh Ross, Graham MacKay, Mrs V. Claspar, Mrs G. Jack.
Front Row: Iona Ross, Peter Haynes, James MacDonald, Florence Haynes, Gary MacDonald, Nicola Gammie, Jayne Haynes, Amy Clark, Linda Jack, Paul Henderson.

Concert rehearsal in the late 1980s
The pupils are wearing sweatshirts with the the TPS Logo

Mrs Clasper initiated the idea of involving parents in running a Bring and Buy sale to raise money for resources and activities. This event evolved into the annual May Fair (although in some recent years it has been a September Fair). It is strongly supported by the local community and is an enjoyable afternoon.

The new Headteacher and her assistant, Margaret Buchanan, set out to make the school into a 'busy place' with every room, corner and corridor used as a learning experience. The corridor was changed from a long pink

Two budding chefs

echoing space into a series of learning centres. A House Corner was set up – complete with a properly wallpapered wall and a mirror to view 'Mr Bun the Baker' where the dressing-up box led to much imaginative role-playing. The computer corner was established and the children used their free access to use the computer tapes – the machine was never off. A peaceful area was established with seats and a tropical fish tank where children could just sit and chat. A cooking section was set out.

Parts of the cloakrooms were converted into libraries and over the years the selection of books was increased. For a time one of the library areas became a resource base. (Recently the other was modified to provide a computer centre.)

Classrooms were reorganised and carpeted. It is interesting that the carpets which were guaranteed for five years were replaced in the summer of 2004, sixteen years later.

School uniform was introduced – red sweatshirts (or black if they wished). The motif, TPS (Tore Primary School), was used to begin with but a few years later *'Growing for the future'* was adopted.

An innovation in 1986 for Primary 5 to 7, in collaboration with the PE teacher, was a trip to the Lecht to ski. For some of the children that was great fun, for others it was an exercise in keeping upright or avoiding someone else's ski pole.

In May that year the children who had left their Primary School in 1982, to go to Fortrose Academy, took part in the new Standard Grade exams in some subjects.

Joanne and Kelly MacRae, whose grandmother and great-grandfather had both attended the school, were pupils in the 1980s. Joanne remembers school being a lot of fun, especially Friday afternoons when, in the good weather, they had activities in the playground. Sometimes this meant sitting painting, at other times they worked in teams – creating models of animals out of any materials they could find.

She also speaks about school outings to exciting places such as Brodie and Dunrobin Castles, and a Barbecue on the beach at the teacher's home at Balblair.

During session **1988-89** part of playground was dug up. Grass was put in and trees were planted. The schoolhouse garden was acquired about the same time.

A team with their elephant made out of 'junk'

1989 will be remembered as the year in which the Berlin wall came down – triggering events which led to the downfall of Communism in Eastern Europe and the Soviet Union.

The United Nations Convention on the Rights of the Child was adopted by the General Assembly in the same year. Within six years it had been ratified by a hundred and eighty nations.

1988-89

Photograph by Andrew Allan

Back Row: Donna MacLean, Rosalind Grant, Joanne MacRae, Scott MacPherson, Ruaraidh Ross, Gary Murray, Philip Balfour, Gregor Jack.
2nd Row: Florence Haynes, John MacKenzie, James Main, Mark Lawson, Nicola Gammie, Kim Fraser, Jayne Haynes.
3rd Row: Ross Fraser, Iona Ross, Wendy Grant, Kelly MacRae, Emma Fraser, Angus Ross, Peter Haynes.
Front Row: Andrew Gardiner.

Christmas art
work

Classroom in
the 1980s

On the beach at
Balblair

New school logo

14. Growing for the Future

A major change in the 1990s was the introduction of Devolved School Management whereby the Education Committees gave headteachers more control of the running of their own schools. This meant that a number of decisions which used to be made by the local authority were now taken at school level (in consultation with the School Board). Recruitment of new staff was increasingly devolved to the school itself, again in consultation with the School Board, and the school had more control of its own budget. Tore School became involved in August 1998.

School Development Plans became mandatory during that decade, with the Headteacher having to present these to the School Board.

At summer 1991 Mrs Elaine MacArthur was appointed as assistant teacher – for the younger pupils – in place of Margaret Buchanan who had retired.

1992

Back Row: Mark Lawson, David Bell, James Main, John MacKenzie, Florence Haynes, Nicola Gammie, Jayne Haynes.

2nd Row: Iona Ross, Wendy Grant, Sarah Bell, Gregor Jack, Emma Fraser, Ross Fraser, Andrew Gardiner.

3rd Row: Eilidh Ross, Scott MacIver, Andrew Fraser, Martin Gammie, Craig Gardiner, Kirsty Lawson, Lindsay Schroeder, Alison Bell.

Front Row: Elise Gammie, Bobby Main, Gemma Bartlett, Elaine Bartlett, Kim Fraser, Martin Bremner, Fiona Roberts.

In January 1992 Gwen Jack retired as dinner-lady and cleaner. She had been in the school since the early 1970s and was very supportive of the staff, involving herself in many aspects of school life. She was also hallkeeper, a task with which she continued until 1997. At the school Julie MacIver took over Gwen's duties until summer 1993 when she was replaced by Shirley Schroeder. Both women had children in the school at the time and they became very involved in the work of the School Board when it was set up in the early 1990s. Jessie MacLennan was appointed as cleaner and dinner-lady when Shirley resigned.

Mrs Clasper retired in 1993 and Mrs Maggie MacLeod was appointed in her place. She came to Tore from Dingwall Primary School. In October 1994 Mrs Sally Thorne took responsibility for the younger classes when Mrs MacArthur became ill. In February 1995 Mrs MacArthur died after some months of illness – a sad time for the staff and pupils. A tree was planted by the children, in her memory, at Killearnan Church.

A School Board was formed during Mrs MacLeod's time and Rev Grant Bell, Free Church minister, was Chairman; Julie MacIver was Secretary.

Mrs MacLeod was instrumental in setting up a five-a-side football team, and she entered teams for orienteering competitions, sometimes held on Ord Hill. The annual fund-raising event expanded into a large fete, the May Fair.

In **1993-94** Mrs MacLeod entered a choir in the Inverness Festival where they came first in their section. Along with the Music teacher she wrote plays for the children – plays which she still uses in her present school.

Children were taken to Aigas House where they made a study of the River Beauly from its source and including the salmon farms. Mrs MacLeod recalls how good the Tore parents were about using their cars to take pupils to football and other events.

In June 1995 the school took first place in a Ross-shire Crime Prevention Project. Scott MacIver and Lindsay Schroeder accepted the prize at a ceremony at the Police HQ in Dingwall.

1995 - 96

Mrs MacLeod left in 1995 to take up an appointment in Hamilton College, an independent school in Lanarkshire, where she is Head of the Junior School. Miss Margo MacLennan, Depute Head in Tarradale, took up duty as Headteacher in January 1996.

Scott and Lindsay (front) with the trophy

Because of very wintry weather the school could not open on the first day so Miss MacLennan had to wait until the next day to meet her new pupils.

*There were only seventeen pupils in the school when I started
– not enough for two full-time teachers, so Sally Thorne took
the infants each morning while I took the upper school, but in
the afternoons, I had all seventeen.*

In February 1996 pupils competed at the Inverness Music Festival. The
Choir was awarded a Certificate of Merit while the Music-making Group
gained first place, winning a trophy. The Choral Verse-speaking Group
gained first place in the small schools section. Eilidh Ross and Fiona Roberts
were first in the Recorder Duet with Elaine Bartlett and Elise Gammie in
second place.

Miss MacLennan initiated weekend trips for the older pupils:

*In 1996 we went to the Strathconon Field Centre but from
1997 we began our annual trips to Ardgour Outdoor Centre on
the Ardnamurchan peninsula.*

The annual May Fair continued and in 1996 retired Headteacher, Rena
Cadger, was invited to open it. That Fair raised over £780, an amazing sum
for a school with less than twenty children. A five-a-side football challenge
with Tarradale primary school was a new feature of the afternoon.

Later in the summer a new musical event was embarked upon – a
Summer Evening of Entertainment. A mixed programme of items was
produced – singing, recorder group, other instrumental groups, plays and so
on, involving the children.

For several years, during Miss
MacLennan's time, the staff and
pupils produced a school and
community magazine, *Talking Tore*,
copies of which were sold at various
local outlets. This publication, which
was popular with pupils and parents
and with the community at large,
contained interesting news about the
school and the locality.

Reunion of Former Pupils
November 1996

A reunion for former pupils (pre-1960 vintage) was attended by a good number
of people. It was an afternoon of reminiscences and information. The children
were fascinated by the stories they were hearing of life at the school
many years before. One lady confessed to an incident when all the

Front: Mrs Val Clasper (left) on her retirement, with Elaine MacArthur
Back: Mrs West (left) and Mrs Janice Jack

pupils, going out for PE (or Drill as it was then called), hid in the bushes. When the teacher arrived there was nobody in sight. They were all given the strap so didn't do that again.

Among those present was the oldest living former pupil at the time – Bessie Tulloch who was ninety-four. She was the second eldest of a family of nine MacLennans (known as 'The Scouts') who had attended the school over the period from 1908 until 1927 when the youngest was transferred, along with several other children, to Mulbuie School to ease the accommodation problems in Tore. At first they had lived at Muckernich but latterly at Newton of Ferintosh from where those children walked to school every day. In May, following the Reunion, Bessie Tulloch was invited to open the May Fair.

Achievements

During session **1996-97** the children (and staff) of Tore School had many achievements. The school had the lowest absentee rate in the Highland Council area and the fourth lowest in all Scotland. In May teachers and pupils were invited to a ceremony in Tulloch Castle Hotel where they received a Highland Council Civic Award in recognition of the school's outstanding contribution to the life of the Community. This was the first time a school had won this award.

There was much musical activity in addition to the usual Christmas and summer

Photograph: SteveBrown

Tore pupils at the award ceremony

shows. A Ceilidh was held in Tore Hall where the children and some outside artistes performed. As a result £160 was donated to the Nansen Society. Pupils (and the Headteacher) entertained at the Hall Committee's Burns Supper. The children produced a music cassette, 'Tore Mix 96'. That resulted in a visit from Arthur Brocklebank, producer of Moray Firth Radio's 'Cadenza', who invited Miss MacLennan and Primary 6/7 to host the two-hour programme on 10th February, giving interviews and chatting about the tape and favourite classical music. For days afterwards people were phoning the school with congratulations.

During the week beginning Monday 3rd February 1997 pupils featured on ITV's 'Reflections' programme with the Rev Susan Brown, minister of Killearnan Church of Scotland and a member of the School Board. Mrs Brown took a very active interest in the work of the school, acting as one of the Chaplains. School services were held in her Church and on at least one occasion the children were treated to lunch by the congregation after the Service.

Mairi Hedderwick, author of the Katie Morag stories and many other books, visited the schoool in February to talk about her writing.

Pupils competed at the 1997 Inverness Music Festival attaining Distinction in Choral Verse-speaking and Group Music-making. Lindsay Schroeder gained a Certificate of Merit for her Vocal Solo in the section for girls aged eleven to fourteen. The Recorder Group played at the Prizewinners Gala Concert in Eden Court and received a standing ovation. At the Easter Ross Mod the school was awarded a certificate as was Lindsay for her individual performance.

Back Row: Mrs S. Thorne, Elise Gammie, Bobby Main, Fiona Roberts, Kirsty Mill, Elaine Bartlett, Miss M. MacLennan, Scott MacIver.
2nd Row: Kirsty Lawson, Martin Gammie, Lindsay Schroeder, Susanne Schroeder, Alison Bell, Eilidh Ross.
3rd Row: Nicky Roberts, Kirstie MacCallum, Stacey Chambers.
Front row: Morven Brown, Tom Bartlett, Samantha Smith, Alasdair Grigor, Stephanie Grant, Alison MacIver, Ewan MacCallum.

The General Purposes room was given a face-lift. A cupboard was built to store, among other things, the canteen tables and benches and so give a safer environment for the children when using that room. A mural for the wall of the cupboard was prepared in lino-cut by the pupils in conjunction with the area's Artist-in-Residence.

Early in 1997 the children of Primary 5-7 started learning French. In preparation for this teachers had been attending courses to prepare them for delivering the course.

At the Inter-School Sports held in Dingwall the school team won their section, gaining thirty-two points, and retained the trophy for a second year.

Kirsty Lawson wrote for *Talking Tore* about the weekend in May at Ardgour.

Ardgour activities Drawing by Kirsty Mill

On Friday 16th May some of the P5-7s went to Ardgour for a school trip. We left the school at 9.50 am and made our way to Fort William for the Corran Ferry to Ardgour. When we got to the Centre we went up and saw our rooms.

The P.7s went abseiling and the P.5-6s did archery, then we swapped over.

After dinner we played Hockey and Rounders. Then (before we went to bed) we sang some songs and had hot chocolate. That night we could not get to sleep because it was so hot.

On Saturday it was not a very nice day. The P.5-6s did orienteering and went on the Adventure Course. Then we swapped over with the P.7s and went gorge walking. We put our water-proofs and helmets on. Miss MacLennan came in the water but when it started to get deeper, she decided to walk along the side. Soon, my legs and Alison Bell's legs got covered in water and we were freezing. Miss MacLennan was calling us two old grannies. When we got back we had a shower. On Sunday, we went canoeing and walked over the hills to the centre again. At 5.30 pm we got the ferry and by quarter to eight we were home!

About two weeks later the younger pupils spent a night at the Girl Guide Centre in the old Killearnan School.

1997 - 98

At the end of September the school held a Ceilidh in Tore Hall. Children, staff and some friends took part in a programme of Scottish music. There were songs and a great variety of instrumental pieces. The event raised £426 for school funds and as a result of a raffle on the evening £165.70 was donated to the Nansen Society. That group of young adults, based at Redcastle Station, works closely with the school.

On the evening of 19th November 1997 the children of Primary 5 to 7 gave an excellent demonstration to parents on the educational use of computers and computer software.

At the Eastgate Centre, the following Saturday, Tore was one of two Black Isle schools (Mulbuie was the other) who sang to raise money for Children 1st – supporting the Family Resource Centre on the Black Isle.

The School Pantomime held in Tore Hall was (and still is) an important event in the school calendar and well-supported by the community as well as family members and friends. That year was no exception when the children put on a performance of Little Red Riding Hood. Successful events such as that represented much hard work on the part of the staff and pupils. Mrs Christine MacLeod, the Music specialist, contibutes to the success of musical events and the children's performances in the Music competitions at the Festival.

Fight for Survival

In November 1997 Highland Council Education Committee embarked on a course of action to save money by closing several schools in its area. This included Tore, along with Mulbuie, Newmore, Achnasheen and Inverasdale in the Ross and Cromarty Division.

The plan was that the pupils of Tore would go to Conon-Bridge or North Kessock, involving them in considerable extra travelling time to and from school. More importantly parents were proud of the achievements of Tore School and highly satisfied with the education their children were receiving there. Local residents could see that were the school to close the one major focal point within the community would be lost. One person wrote in a letter to the *North Star*:

> When a school is removed from a community that community dies a slow death. So many rural activities take place in and around the school.....

Parents were galvanised into action to fight the closures. An Action Group was formed and battle commenced.

> The situation is very serious. The school is the heart of the Tore Community. If it were to close this would have a very much wider impact. We will fight Council proposals EVERY INCH OF THE WAY and will take our fight to the Scottish Office or higher if we have to.

Evelyn Brown who was Chair of the school Board at the time, wrote in a Press Release of 11th November 1997:

> The school is a flagship for the excellence which can flow from rural schools. The most recent School Inspectors' report concluded with "Tore Primary School has a strong base from which to continue to improve its provision in the years to come." Even from abroad the standards are marvelled at. Indeed, Ellen Powey, Doctoral candidate in Educational Leadership at Brigham Young University in Utah commented recently that Tore was unique in its standards, approach and successes. Tore school is small but it achieves a lot.

A Newsletter, *Growing for the Future*, was launched on 17th November 1997 to keep parents informed of progress.

Meetings with the other threatened schools were held. There seemed to be an endless supply of strategies to make their voice heard by the powers that be – from Mrs MacIver, Chairperson of the Education Committee to

Donald Dewar, the then Secretary of State for Scotland (and who later became First minister in the devolved Scottish Parliament). Parents lobbied Brian Wilson who was Scottish Office Minister for Education at the time. Every week the local papers published articles and photographs of the school's activities and the continuing achievements of the children.

Signs and leaflets were produced and all over the area **Save our Schools** posters appeared on trees, poles, wheelie bins and so on.

One of Tore's most effective publicity stunts was the creation of an eye-catching bale tableau with frequently-changing slogans in a field near the roundabout.

The photograph below shows Calum Dalgetty and Stuart Gammie with

their Dads who constructed the *sculpture*. The picture is symbolic. These two little preschoolers represented the pupils of the future for whom, along with those currently attending, the school had to be saved. Stuart and Calum were due to finish Primary 7 at the end of Session 2004 - 2005, completing their elementary education in a school which, had the Council accomplished their aim, would not have survived to complete one hundred and twenty-five years.

Letters from all sectors of the community (and far beyond) appeared in the newspapers and were sent to MPs, Councillors, the Prime Minister. Charles Kennedy, MP for Ross, Cromarty and Skye, took up the cause and visited Tore School.

On 16th December a joint protest march took place through Inverness from the Spectrum Centre (also nominated for closure) to the Highland Council Buildings. A Council meeting on the 18th decided that the matter of closures should go to consultation.

The Tore School Action Group produced a video showing the work of the school and its involvement in the community and a copy was sent to members of the Education Committee. At Christmas, just a few weeks after the news broke, a Christmas card was sent to all Councillors.

A group of parents and Highland Councillors went to Edinburgh on 14th April 1998 to lobby at the Scottish Office and, on Thursday 23rd April, a feature on the schools appeared in the *North Star*.

> *Every school is important to its community. Today education councillors meet to decide the future of the ten Highland primary schools threatened with closure.*

Several members of the newspaper's editorial team went behind the scenes at each of the schools.

> *They ask why they should be kept open. They discover what each school means to the parents, pupils and local residents. And they find that there is logic and emotion in their arguments.*

From Tore we wish you Christmas Cheer
And health and joy for the New Year.
Our happy smiles conceal our fear
That next New Year we won't be here.

We've won awards and great acclaim
We're up for closure all the same
What we achieve is often praised
Is all our work to be erased?

Whatever powers-that-be may say
We dread two long bus-rides each day.
Our school's the village heart and core
Without the school there'll be no Tore

So, as the controversy soars
Will you vote to support our cause?
Should village schools now close their doors?
(Next time that village might be yours).

From Tore we wish you Christmas Cheer
And conscience clean for the New Year.

Thank you

The front (top) and inside of the Christmas card.

The message from Clare Blois, spokeswoman for Tore, was:

I would like to say to them that we would like common sense to prevail. We all know the facts, we have listened to them and we hope they have listened to us....
The councillors should have the common sense to see the detrimental effect the closure would have on the children and the community.

And they had. That day the Education Committee voted against the closure of Tore and also Mulbuie, Newmore, Inverasdale. There was one more hurdle – the full Council meeting on 7th May. But there was much celebration when at that meeting the Council ratified the Education Committee's decision and also voted against the closure of Achnasheen.

In spite of all the uncertainty the work at school had being going on as usual. Children were learning and achieving. At the Inverness Music Festival in February two girls performed well in Verse-speaking: Alison MacIver gained Distinction in her group and Susanne Schroeder gained Merit in hers.

Photograph: Steve Brown

In the Spring the older pupils organised a Car Wash to raise funds for their trip to Ardgour.

There was also a Coffee Morning and Bring and Buy Sale which raised almost £240 for Arthritis Research and a Blue Peter Appeal.

The pupils of Primary 5 to 7 made the trip to Kyle on Scotrail's 'Travelling Classroom' which seemed to be an interesting experience. All the children received a fax-file and a badge: '*Stay off the line and stay alive.*'

The school took part in a Spring Clean Campaign and filled twelve black bags with rubbish from around the Tore area.

Alison MacIver, a Primary 5 pupil, won first prize in a competition to design a coat of arms and logo for Tesco as part of their 'Computers for Schools' programme.

For three weeks in April/May Fiona Jamieson, a student at Northern College, carried out her rural schools placement at Tore.

The pupils of Primary 1 to 4 visited Groam House Museum in Rosemarkie and went for a walk up the Fairy Glen. As part of their 'Pond Life' project they made trips to Aigas Field Centre, Culbokie Wood and the Nansen Pond. The children in Primary 5 to 7, as part of their 'Woodlands' topic, visited Aldourie Wood, Dores, and the Stratosphere and Hazlehead Park in Aberdeen.

In early May Primary 7, who were studying the topic of the Highland Clearances, visited Dunrobin Castle and then went on to Dornoch Cathedral where Susan Brown, formerly of Killearnan, is minister.

1998-99

Back Row: Stacey Chambers, Katharine MacKenzie, Kirsty Lawson, Alison Bell, Nicky Roberts.
2nd Row: Samantha Smith, Susanne Schroeder, Morven Brown, Alison MacIver, Kirstie MacCallum, Ewan MacCallum,Stephanie Grant.
Front Row: Kirsty Egan, Gregor Williamson, Caitlin Orr, Morven-May MacCallum, Alasdair Grigor, Katie Blois.

Celebrating survival!

At the Primary Inter-school Sports in June the school team gained first place in their Group (H). In a School Security competition they were awarded second place.

In June 1998, for the first time since 1707, Scotland had its own Parliament. A referendum had been held in September 1997 when the people of Scotland voted in favour of devolved Parliament. Donald Dewar was appointed First Minister.

1998 - 99

Margo's Army of Dads (MAD)

Photograph: Steve Brown

Around this time fathers of the pupils were encouraged to become involved in doing odd jobs around the school – from digging the hole for the time capsule to putting up fences and painting windowsills. Since that time they have been very active and have carried out many tasks.

With the threat of closure lifted the pupils buried a time capsule in the playground in November 1998. Among the items included were newspaper clippings regarding the closures, written articles from the children, a Tore School teatowel and a Tore School sweatshirt. A plaque which marks the spot tells that it is due to be dug up in 2048.

TIME CAPSULE
Buried by Tore Pupils
7th October 1998
To be Exhumed
7th October 2048

The teatowel was produced to raise funds. The children drew pictures of themselves (and their teachers) and wrote their names. They were then all printed on the teatowel.

More successes

At the Inverness Festival in February 1999 pupils from the school performed very well and many were placed including Tom McKenna who was first in Solo Verse-speaking for pupils of Primary 1/2 and Kirstie MacCallum who took first place in the Primary 4/5 section. The younger pupils won their Choral Verse-speaking and the older pupils' Music-making Group also gained first place.

A School Board meeting in February discussed the matter of storage space and problems associated with the increased roll. In comments reminiscent of the early 1900s and the 1920s the Headteacher pointed out that the junior classroom was becoming short of space and the GP room was proving too small for the whole class to join together for activities such as Drama. Changing shoes in the front lobby was becoming difficult. Consideration had to be given as to how these problems could be overcome.

During the session the pupils became involved with the 'Wayfarers' Project (for the Millennium) in which, under the supervision of the late Dr Kerr Yule of Ross and Cromarty Heritage Society, schools collected and submitted material for a multi-media account of their community.

Alison Bell won Office International's 'Design a cover' schools competition, winning a personal CD player and £250 worth of stationery for the school. The comment from her classmates:*'What a prize!'*

In April the pupils of Primary 4 to 7 were given the opportunity to participate in football coaching at Ross County's Victoria Park with Steven Munro, the Assistant Community Coach.

For several weeks of the summer term Hayley Walsh, from Inverness, carried out her Rural Schools placement (teaching practice) at the school. About the same time members of staff from Fortrose Academy visited the Primary 7 pupils in preparation for their transition to the Academy.

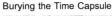
Burying the Time Capsule

Back Row: Miss M. MacLennan, Alison Bell, Mrs Jessie MacLennan, Alison MacIver, Susanne Schroeder, Nicki Roberts, Christopher King, Mrs Trish MacGregor, Peter McKenna, Mrs Sally Thorne, Alexander Thorne.
2nd Row: Morven Brown, Samantha Smith, Alasdair Grigor, Tom McKenna, Kirsty MacLennan, Caitlin Orr, Katie Blois, Siobhan King.
3rd Row: Daisy Hewitt, Stuart Gammie, Rachel King, Calum Dalgetty, Gregor Williamson, Kirsty Egan.
Front: Kerry Williamson, Claire Rae, Alastair Coote, Amber Brown.

15. Into the 21st Century

At the beginning of session **1999 - 2000** the Headteacher put forward the idea of parental involvement in activities in the school. Crafts, sewing, cooking, games, computer supervision were some of those mentioned.

A sign of the deterioration of trust in society generally, and among people working with children in particular, was the fact that any parents volunteering would have to undergo Scottish Criminal Records Office checks. And at this time, as a result of incidents in some schools, security systems became mandatory.

In October 1999 the school children (one from each class) were helped by the Nansen Society to plant a Millennium garden in the village. According to Kirstie MacCallum of Primary 6: *'We planted daffodils and other flowers.....We planted some trees and had our photo taken. ...we went back to Tore school after having a great muddy time gardening.'*

Millennium

As 1999 drew to a close and 2000 began celebrations were held to welcome a new millennium and the 21st Century. Although there was disagreement as to whether 2000 or 2001 should be considered the first year of the century the world celebrated the new millennium on 1st January 2000.

*(Note: The **20th** Century had not officially begun until 1st January 1901).*

Tore School parents organised an event with a bonfire and fireworks followed by a party in the Hall. Morven Brown, a Primary 6 pupil at the time, wrote an account of the way they greeted the new Millennium.

> *It was great fun. At about 11.45 we did the last Strip the Willow of 1999. I was beginning to get very excited. The last minute of 1999 was being counted. The D.J. brought a TV which showed London and Big Ben. We then sang Auld Lang Syne and did the first Strip the Willow of 2000. There were balloons on the roof which were let down.*

Later in the year a millennium medal, designed by pupil Alison MacIver, was presented to all the children at school. Alison's design, which depicts the roundabout at Tore, had been chosen as the prizewinner in a competition at the 1999 May Fair.

Accommodation

During the late 1990s, with the future of the school secure and its reputation spreading as a centre of excellence, placing requests began to be received from outside the catchment area. At their January 2000 meeting members of the School Board agreed that the steadily rising school roll and number and frequency of such placing requests were cause for serious concern. In the light of the current accommodation there was the fear that the school

Tore School's
Millennium Medal

might not have places for families moving into the area.

By May the maximum recommended capacities of rooms were confirmed at twenty for each classroom and twenty-two for the GP room. If the total reached forty-four pupils the school would qualify for another half-time teacher and at forty-eight another full-time teacher would be appointed.

The schoolhouse was 'given' by the Council to the school as additional accommodation. Various plans for its renovation and use have been considered but by 2004 nothing had been decided. By June 2000 an additional classroom (demountable unit) was looking likely.

Activities

There were several successes at the 2000 Inverness Music Festival, including a Distinction and the award of the Northern Meeting Trophy for their Action Song, a Distinction in Choral Verse-speaking for the children of Primary 1, 2 and 3. Also on the Music front Kirstie and Morven-May MacCallum sang at the Easter Ross Mod in May. Kirstie gained first place in solo singing.

The Parents' Association continued to work very hard with fund-raising events and in 2000 they produced a Recipe book.

At the May 2000 Swimming Gala at Alness Academy, Tore was first in Group D out of seven small schools. They won the Scotsburn Shield.

As part of their work on the topics, 'The Seashore' and 'In and Around the Moray Firth', the pupils were taken to Rosemarkie Beach where they carried out a variety of activities including identifying different types of beach life, looking at rock pools and making a survey of what was found in the various tidal zones. The children found all sorts of sea creatures.

An educational event for Primary 7 took place at the Cameron Barracks in Inverness. A presentation was given on safety in areas such as train tracks, tractors, the sea, building sites and others.

At the Inter-school Sports Peter McKenna, Jessica Clayton and Alison MacIver gained points for the Tore team. Alison was placed first in three events – 100m, 150 m and long jump. The PE specialist then was Graham Calder who, in March, had taken Mrs Eileen Mackenzie's place when she had to take time off because of illness.

Around this time Mr Macdonald who had been Headteacher from 1964 to 1973 paid a visit to the school. He took with him poems which his pupils had written as part of their projects.

A survey carried out this year among the pupils to find their favourite subjects indicated that Art was by far the most popular.

Art Award 2002

Part of the Project, 'Terrific Tore Tales',
which won the
Artworks: Young Artist of the Year Award

In London: John MacNaught Artist-in-Residence and Miss MacLennan with the three pupils who were chosen to go to receive the Award

Mrs Marion Tonkin, the specialist Art teacher, visits weekly inspiring the children and helping foster artistic creativity.

2000-01

Mrs Kate Paulin was appointed Classroom Assistant to help Mrs Thorne in her room with Primary 1 and 2 for five hours per week. The allocation of time for the specialist Music teacher was cut from one visit per week to one per fortnight.

In January 2001, because of the increasing roll, Mrs Maisie Mackenzie was appointed to help Jessie MacLennan with school lunches. Maisie has had a long connection with the school since her eldest child began as a pupil in 1958 right through until her youngest left in 1995.

The deployment of parent helpers began in February 2000 when Needlework was introduced, followed by computer work in the summer. At Easter 2001 Mrs Thorne took maternity leave and Mrs Eva MacKenzie was appointed to cover her classes for the summer term.

It was decided around this time that, for security reasons, the school gate should be kept shut at all times during school hours.

2001-02

By August 2001 the new (demountable) classroom with a corridor linking it to the main building was completed. Miss MacLennan with Primary 4 to 7 occupied the new unit while Primary 1 to 3 continued to use the west room. A door had been opened between that room and the middle one so that the younger classes had a playroom. Miss Moira Dillon was appointed to teach Mrs Thorne's classes in place of Mrs MacKenzie.

The school session began with the acquisition of a new football pitch in part of Kenny MacLennan's field beside the school. This was required to compensate for the loss of a large area of playground where the new classroom was sited.

At a School Board meeting in December 2001 Jim Holden was elected Chairman in place of Clare Blois whose term as a Board member had come to an end. She had chaired the Board since March 2000. There was ongoing debate about the incorporation of the schoolhouse and the urgency of finding somewhere to house an allocation of new computers. Another matter which had been before the School Board for several years was the need for a covered area at the front door of the school to provide shelter for the children.

During the autumn term work began on a project to decorate the new link corridor with artwork inspired by the history of the Parish. The pupils worked with John MacNaught, Artist-in-Residence with the Council's Culture and Leisure Department.

This Project, 'Terrific Tore Tales', won the *Artworks: Young Artist of the Year Award*, the first school in Scotland to do so. Their award was in the category 'Working with Artists' and three of the children were picked, by ballot, to attend the awards ceremony at Tate Modern in London in June 2002.

The visit included a special tour of the works of art in the State Dining Room of Buckingham Palace.

The Award was £2000 for the school and a signed limited-edition print from world-famous artist Anish Kapoor. In addition £50 was given to the school so that the other pupils could share in an event to celebrate National Children's Art Day.

Early in June 2002 schools were given a holiday to mark the Queen's Golden Jubilee.

2002 - 03

During the summer holidays, on July 26th, Miss MacLennan's marriage to Leonard Fraser took place.

The school roll was up to fifty in August and Miss Dillon was appointed as full time teacher for Primary 1 to 3. Mrs Thorne, job-sharing with Mrs Morven Hulks who was appointed in October, taught Primary 4/5 and Margo Fraser was responsible for Primary 6/7.

Over the summer the new computer suite was installed in one of the library areas. Visits from the PE specialist were reduced from weekly to fortnightly. Since Tore was allocated the Drama specialist, Mrs Ann Mardon, only on alternate years staff were expected to deliver the Drama courses every other year and there was now the fear that the time for Art and Music specialists might also be reduced. At this time a Pupils' Council was formed with representatives from each class to put forward suggestions. Two older pupils from the Council attended the early part of School Board meetings.

Because of the increased number of children in the school the Christmas production was in three parts – one from each classroom. To accommodate all those who wished to attend there were performances over two evenings.

In March 2003 at the Inverness Festival the school gained three Certificates of Merit: for the performance of the Recorder Group, an Action Song by the children of Primary 1 to 3 and the Music-making Group. The pupils of Primary 4/5 won the Group Verse-speaking with Distinction. Katie Blois won the Flute section for her age group.

A new idea for the school's Policy on Promoting Positive Behaviour was the introduction of Golden Time. A period of twenty-five minutes was to be set aside on Friday afternoon for extra playtime or other activities of the children's choice. It was linked to adherence to the Golden Rules which were drawn up by the pupils themselves through the School Council.

There were several outings in the summer term, in addition to the annual trip to Ardgour for Primary 6/7. The children of Primary 1 to 3 spent a day at the Aigas Field centre and Primary 4/5 visited Rothiemurchus Estate and the Tor Achilty Dam.

Tutors from Feis Rois took Primary 1 to 3 for lessons in Gaelic Singing.

Tore Primary School

'SUMMER EVENING OF ENTERTAINMENT'

Tuesday 25th June 2002 at 7. 00 p.m. – Tore Hall

1) 'Pirate Adventure' – P.1 - 4

2) **Guitar groups** (Beginners & Improvers)
Klrsty, Gregor & Daisy – 'Kum ba Yah' & 'Swing Low Sweet Chariot';
Katy, Caitlin & Alex - 'The Wombling Song', 'Streets of London' & 'Flower of Scotland'.

3) The 'Torchestra'
Claire, Kirsty, Katy, Caitlin, Samantha & Kerry – 'Five well-known tunes';

4) A selection of songs from P.1 – 4;

5) Special guest appearance by new local band;

6) *P.7 Presentation* (incl. Cycling proficiency badges & certificates for P.5 – 7)

7) **Beginners' Recorder Group**
Keir, Morven, Jack, Amber & Angela – 'The Birdie Song'

8) **P.4 – 7 topic playlets**
(i) 'I don't know why you're still smoking' by Tomas Storey;
(ii) 'The Smoke Team vs. Tore' by Jack Evans;
(iii) 'Stop smoking! It kills you! (I'm not joking!) by Rowan Moore;
(iv) 'Smoke, smoke & more smoke!' by Amber Brown

9) *'Artworks'* **competition presentation** by John McNaught

10) – **Whole school**
'If I were a butterfly......'

There will be a collection at the door for the NSPCC – please give generously.

The senior pupils who took part in the annual Swimming Gala at Alness Academy retained the Scotsburn Trophy when they gained first place in their section.

In June Mrs Kate Paulin, classroom assistant, left to take up a full time post at Coulhill Primary School, Alness. Mrs Morag Coburn became Support for Learning auxiliary until June 2004.

The annual end-of-term Summer Evening of Entertainment took place on 2nd July.

2003 - 04

This session was characterised by staff changes. Mrs Trish MacGregor, Learning Support auxiliary, left to take up an appointment in Dingwall Academy in August. The school secretary, Mrs Jackie Leitch, left in September and was replaced by Mrs Dorothy Morrison.

In October 2003 Mrs Margo Fraser resigned. The Authority then decided that Tore and Ferintosh Schools should share a Headteacher who would have no class commitment. The scheme was already being piloted in a cluster of schools in Skye. In the interim Mrs Mary Deverill acted as Headteacher and class teacher of Primary 6/7.

Mrs Jenny Wilson was appointed Headteacher for the two schools in January 2004 and when she took up this appointment Jillian MacDonald joined the staff as class teacher for Primary 6/7. About the same time Mrs Jane Rosie was appointed classroom assistant and Gail Robertson, a student teacher, spent some time on placement in the school.

Festival successes have continued. Sports and extra-curricular activities are strong. Mrs Morven Hulks runs Scripture Union alternating with 'Beatz' (a singing group). Mrs Anne MacIntyre trains a Recorder Group and badminton, coached by Elaine Murray, takes place weekly. The children also have the opportunity to learn to play a Brass instrument under the tuition of Mrs Hook.

The local ministers, Rev Iain Ramsden of the Church of Scotland and Rev Douglas MacKeddie of the Free Church, regularly visit the school as their predecessors did and school services are held at the end of each term.

Having lunch at Killearnan Church after a school service

For several years the pupils have been involved in preparing shoeboxes of gifts for children in Eastern Europe. These are collected and transported abroad by Blythswood Care.

August 2004

Although at the beginning of 2004-05 the school roll went down, a large number of the pupils still come from outwith the school catchment area. Miss Dillon was appointed in 2004 to Support for Learning and now attends Tore School only one day each week. Miss MacDonald then moved to Primary 1 to 3 and Miss Megan Beaumont who belongs to Tasmania was appointed for 6 and 7. (Miss MacDonald recently married and is now Mrs Quigley.)

Mrs Thorne was seconded from August 2004 for a year to teach Technology and Science at Strathpeffer, Tore and Conon-Bridge. Mrs Margaret Berry was appointed to cover her class commitment in Tore and, also in August, Isobel Rae was appointed Support for Learning auxiliary.

Highlighting the development of new technology, a TV/video/DVD package was bought in 2004. Resources have come a long way since 1879 when there was scarcely a text book. We wonder what 19th Century children would think of the equipment and opportunities available to their descendants today.

Christmas production 2004

16. One hundred and twenty-five years

In October 2004 Tore School completed one hundred and twenty-five years of state education. Hundreds of children (over nine hundred by 1941) have sat in the classrooms there. Each generation has had its memories: some happy, some sad and some which they would sooner forget.

What happened to those children? They scattered far and wide and their descendants are to be found in most countries of the world. It was not the lure of foreign places which drew those early emigrants but the necessity of finding work. Family business, croft or farm could make a living for only a few members of a large family.

Since the days when domestic service or work related to agriculture seemed to be the main sources of employment for youngsters in a rural community Tore School former pupils have found their way into a wide variety of trades and professions.

Schools boast their famous and infamous pupils. There are few 'big names' from Tore School yet all yesterday's children will have, in their own way, left their imprint on society.

Neil Macleod, a former pupil, visited the school a few years ago in his capacity as HMI. He has written:

> *My return to the school to inspect it was indeed an interesting and enjoyable experience. Obviously staff had changed, toilets were now inside instead of outside and the quality and quantity of resources had increased dramatically! Gone were the rigid rows of desks typical of our old school days. They had been replaced by the friendlier, grouped tables conducive with today's learning methodologies. Essentially the character of the building had not changed and many memories of my time in Tore came nostalgically flooding back. It was pleasing to find that the quality of education offered in Tore School was as high as I remembered my own days in the school to be. Despite the long period away from the area, the teachers were able to point out the offspring of those I had known myself, providing yet another pleasing link with the past.*

Links with the Past

Several of the present pupils are the fourth generation of their family to be educated in Tore School.

John MacLennan and Christina Nairne attended Tore School in the early 1900s. He lived at Muckernich and her family lived at Ryefield. They married in 1929 and their son Ian and daughter Chrisanne were pupils of the thirties. Ian's family, David and Isobel, Graham, Julie and Alistair, also attended the school and David's sons, Rory and Neil, are now pupils there. Isobel (Mrs Rae) has been employed in the school as an auxiliary and her children, Claire and Alan, are pupils. Julie (Mrs Chambers) has two daughters with Tore School connections: Stacey is a former pupil but Kathleen is still there. Julie herself has recently been helping out in the school.

Calum and Megan Dalgetty's father, John, was a pupil of the sixties and their grandfather, also John, was the one who, in the thirties, left his slate in the burn all weekend. The story is told in Chapter 7. Their great-grandfather, Willie-John, enrolled in Tore School in1905. Calum and Megan are also great-grandchildren of John and Christina MacLennan.

Hannah Bain's great-grandfather, Donald, was enrolled in 1919, nine of his siblings having already attended the school from 1898. Donald's family, Sandra and Ian, are both former pupils as are Ian's sons, Garry (Hannah's father) and David. So Hannah and her little sister, Megan, who is due to start in 2005, are the fourth generation of their family to be educated there.

Tore School goes on 'Growing for the Future'. Over the past few years since it was threatened with closure it has become a desirable school where parents want to send their children. Under good leadership it has earned an enviable reputation. But we would not like to see it become a victim of its own success. Many of the desirable characteristics arise from the fact that 'small is beautiful'.

In a few years today's infants will be society's adults. What do we wish for them? A better, more secure future? History reveals that each age has its own particular problems and we are sure that the current generation of Tore pupils will be as well equipped for the future as their predecessors were.

Postscript

In December 2004 Mrs Wilson resigned in view of the family's forthcoming move to South Africa. Miss Beaumont was appointed acting Headteacher in the interim. Since Mrs Quigley was due to have maternity leave, Susan Sharkey was appointed in January to teach Primary 1, 2 and 3. About the same time Mrs Audrey Sutherland was appointed as PE specialist.

Mrs Lynne Caddell *(right)* was appointed Headteacher for Tore and Ferintosh as successor to Mrs Wilson and took up her appointment in the summer term 2005.

Staff and Pupils 2004

Staff: Mrs Skillin, Mrs Morag Coburn, Miss Moira Dillon, Mrs Jenny Wilson, Mrs Sally Thorne, Miss Jillian MacDonald, Mrs Jessie MacLennan.

Photograph by Tempest Photography

Pupils 2004/2005

As Tore School completed its hundred and twenty-fifth session
of state education,
the following pupils were in the school.

Hannah Bain, Jordan Black, Katie Blois, Amber Brown, Kathleen Chambers, Alastair Coote, Hannah Coote, Calum Dalgetty, Megan Dalgetty, Drew Drummond, Kirsty Egan, Jack Evans, William Fraser, Hannah Gaitens, Stuart Gammie, Erraid Gaskell, Iona Gaskell, Reiff Gaskell, Rowan Gaskell, Geordie Gladwyn, Imogen Gladwyn, Angela Gray, Thomas Gray, Fraser Grigor, Keir Goodwin, Conor Heafey, Daisy Hewitt, Molly Hewitt, Stuart Hillis, Paul Holden, Joanna Hulks, Craig Kennedy, Sarah Kennedy, Tracey Kennedy, Yolanda Labanca, Zak Labanca, Morven May MacCallum, Anna MacDonald, Stephanie McConnell MacKenzie, Katherine McKenna, Ashley MacLennan, Neil MacLennan, Rory MacLennan, Toni MacLeod, Cory Miller, Kelsey Miller, Caitlin Orr, Christopher Orr, Alex Peasey, Alan Rae, Claire Rae, Gregor Riggs, Ryan Ross, Connor Shewan, Naomi Smith, Calum Stewart (P3), Calum Stewart (P7), T'omas Storey, Alexander Thorne, Gregor Williamson, Kerry Williamson.

They were joined in August 2004 by:

Emma Gray, Jamie Heafey, Rhia MacKenzie, Erin Macleod, Kane Miller and later by Lizzie Lister and Hannah Lister.

In the session beginning August 2005
those in the new Primary 1 class are:

Megan Bain, Ruairidh Fraser, Freya Shepherd, Niamh Shewan.

Population Table

In November 1935 Mr Murray, the Headmaster, drew up a population table to show the number of children in the school. He had two categories: Permanent and Floating. The children in the Permanent category were those who had never attended any other school except Tore while the Floating category included those who had come from other schools.

Class	Permanent	Floating	Total
Infant Jr	3	5	8
Infant Sr	8	0	8
Class I	4	1	5
Class II	9	5	14
Class III	3	2	5
Class IV	3	4	7
Class V	10	9	19
Total	**40**	**26**	**66**

More than one third of the children had already attended at least one other school. There were three main factors contributing to this: farm workers frequently changed their employer; travelling people camped in the area and moved on at certain times of the year; there was a large number of boarded-out children fostered in this area.

School Roll

The chart below gives a rough idea of the way the school roll fluctuated over the past hundred and twenty-five years. Since not every teacher recorded annually the number of pupils, for certain years it has been necessary to interpolate. Other years showed variation in the roll from month to month, May and November being months when sometimes the population of the school changed dramatically. For these years I have attempted to average out the roll.

It is worth bearing in mind that in the 1920s and 1930s there were more than seven classes in the school.

School Roll 1879 to 2004

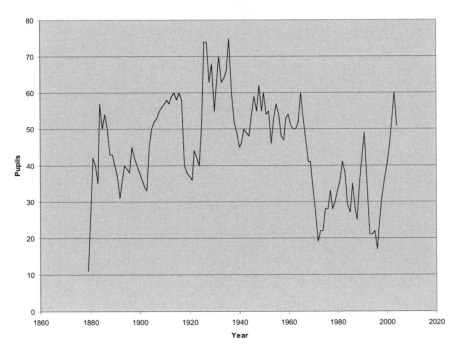

School Roll 1879 to 2004

Teachers 1879 to 2005

October 1879 - 1881	John Tuach
October 1881 - 1883	Helen Stewart
April 1883 - 1885	Williamina Watson
June 1885 - 1886	Jane A. Middleton
1886 - 1890	Jessie Forbes
Oct 1890 - Nov 1901	Helen Macdonald
Nov 1901 - Feb 1902	Miss Macleod, Miss I. H. Macdonald
Feb 1902 - 1904	Helen Macdonald (reappointed)
Oct 1903 - 1904	Elsie Boyne assistant teacher
April 1904 - 1920	James Forrest (Headmaster)
Nov 1909 - 1915	Christina Ann MacLennan
June 1915 - ?	Miss Duncan
? - May 1919	Mrs Hutchison
May 1919 - Nov 1922	Jessie MacKenzie
April 1920 - Sep 1926	Donald MacLeod (Headmaster)
During 1922	Katherine MacLeod (supply)
Jan 1923 - Dec 1930	Jessie MacGregor
During 1925	Miss M. G. Nicholson, Fodderty (supply)
Sep to Dec 1925	Miss C. F. MacKenzie (supply)
Sep 1926 - Jan 1927	Miss M. E. Napier
Nov 1926 - July 1930 and March 1931 - Nov 1938	Janetta H. MacLennan
? 20s / 30s	Miss Davidson (Drill)
Jan 1927 - Sep 1939	Angus Murray (Headmaster)
Sep 1927 (3 weeks)	Cecilia Murray (student)
Dec 1930	Miss Munro
6th Jan 1931- July 1940	Isabella M. Pirie (acting Head from Sep. 1939)
30s	Miss Paterson (Drill)
? 30s / 40s	Miss MacKay (Music)
Sep 1939 - 1946	Miss Reid (acting Headteacher)
Aug 1940 - 1950	Donella Gillies
40s	Mary MacKenzie (supply)
Aug 1946 - 1956	Norman Macleod (Headmaster)
Sep 1955 (3 weeks)	Jean Murray (student)
1956 (summer term)	Grace MacNab
Aug 1950 - 1986	Rena Cadger (Headteacher 1972 - 1986)
Aug 1956 - 1963	Alasdair U. Mackenzie (Headmaster)
June 1962 (1 week)	Isabel MacIver (student)
Sep 1963 (3 weeks)	Sandra Bain (student)

Jan 1964 - 1972	Iain Macdonald (Headmaster)
Sep 1964 (3 weeks)	Christine Hutcheson (student)
1954 - ?	Mrs Cecilia Gray (Music)
1965 - 66	Mrs MacInnes
From mid 50s	Bunty MacFarquhar (supply)
1973 - 79	Margaret Noble
Aug 1979 - 84	Dorothy Morrison
1984	Mrs Kinnear
1984	Mrs Innes (supply)
Aug 1984 - 1991	Margaret Buchanan
Aug 1986 - 1993	Val Clasper (Headteacher)
70s / 80s	Janice Jack
1991 - 1994	Elaine MacArthur
Aug 1993 - Dec 1995	Maggie MacLeod (Headteacher)
Oct 1994 -	Sally Thorne (on secondment August 2004 to 2005)
Jan 1996 - Oct 2003	Margo MacLennan now Mrs Fraser (Headteacher)
April/May 1998	Fiona Jamieson (student)
April/ May 1999	Hayley Walsh (student)
2001 (summer term)	Eva MacKenzie
Aug 2001 - 2004	Moira Dillon (now Support for Learning)
Oct 2002 -	Morven Hulks
Oct 2003 - Feb 2004	Mary Deverill (acting Headteacher)
Feb 2004 - December 2004	Jenny Wilson (Headteacher)
Feb 2004 -	Jillian Macdonald (now Mrs Quigley)
Jan 2005 - Spring 2005	Megan Beaumont (acting Headteacher)
Aug 2004 - 2005	Margaret Berry
Jan 2005 -	Susan Sharkey
April 2005 -	Lynne Caddell (Headteacher)

Additional Supply teachers
Ann MacKenzie, Lilian Campbell, Ishbel MacArthur, Anne MacKay, Muriel Jack, Fiona Fraser, Mrs K. Morrison, Marjory Miller.

Music teachers
Miss Bassin (Organiser), Miss MacKay, Mrs Down, Miss Penny, Mrs Gray, Mr Curr (Organiser), Mrs West, Mrs MacLeod.

Art teachers
Mr Campbell (Adviser), Mr Dunn, Mrs Tonkin.

PE teachers
Miss Davidson, Miss Paterson, Ian Grant, Donald Patience, Miss MacLeman, Mrs Cattanach, Mrs Anderson, Jock Watt, Mrs MacMillan, Eileen MacKenzie, Graham Calder, Mrs Woodhouse, Jared Simpson, Audrey Sutherland.

Sewing teachers
Lydia Munro, Jean Ainslie, Mrs Beveridge.

Remedial/Learning Support
Joey MacRae, Mrs Thomas, Mrs Campbell.

In Memoriam

Time like an ever-rolling stream bears all its sons away

Since the book was begun, about two years ago, several former pupils and others closely connected with the school have sadly passed away.
Below is a list of those we know about. There may be others so I apologise to relatives for any omissions.

Alick Macleod .... September 2003
Bill Srail .... October 2003
Jessie Dalgetty (Mrs Allan) .... December 2003
Douglas Dalgetty .... February 2004
Donald Bain .... August 2004
Barbara Johnstone (Mrs Rose) .... September 2004
Tom Paterson .... October 2004
Gwen Jack (Staff) .... October 2004
Anne MacKenzie (Mrs Hall) .... March 2005
Chrisanne MacLennan (Mrs MacKenzie) .... April 2005
Archie Kirk .... June 2005
Margaret A. MacLean (Mrs Hutcheson) .... June 2005
Jessie MacLennan (Staff) .... July 2005

Inscription on James Forrest's Grave

In Memory
of
James Forrest
Schoolmaster at Tore
Died 21st January 1936 aged 83
also his mother
Ann Johnstone
died 10th May 1907 aged 80

Down the Years

Back: Jimmy Sutherland, Frankie Black, Willie Gammie, ___, Donald Sutherland.
Front: Mr Murray, Hugh Forsyth, Catherine MacLeod, Ina Fraser, Helen Black, ___ John MacRae

Headteacher Margo MacLennan, front, right, pictured with fellow teacher Moira Dillon and the pupils of Tore Primary

Books

Killearnan The Story of the Parish by Mrs Margaret Oag
Killearnan by Susan Thompson
Reminscences by John Macleod
Tales and Travels of a School Inspector by John Wilson
Education in Scotland by Ian R. Findlay
Going to School by Donald Withrington
History of Scottish Education Volumes I & II by James Scotland.
Education in the North Aberdeen College of Education
The Schools at Work published by National Union of Teachers.
The Statistical Account of Scotland
The New Statistical Account of Scotland
Oliver & Boyd's Edinburgh Almanac 1888 and 1892
Easter Ross 1750 - 1850 The Double Frontier by Ian R. Mowat

Resources

Encyclopedia Britannica CD ROM
Kilcoy Papers – Aberdeen University Special Library
School Log Books (Tore and Killearnan)
Valuation Rolls
Redcastle Free Church Records pre-1900 – Free Church of Scotland
Genealogical information: www. scotlandspeople.com
and Inverness Public Library

Acknowledgements

I would like to thank everyone who gave me so much of their time and loaned materials and photographs to compile this book. There are far too many to list each one separately but most of the names appear in the book. If anyone has been omitted, please accept my apologies. Of the others, I would like to express my gratitude to:

Donnie Maclean of Lewis Recordings for all his support and advice.

Isobel MacCallum, Councillor, Knockbain and Killearnan Ward.

Highland Council Archives staff – Bob Steward and Fiona Macleod.

For permission to quote from their publications: Caroline Rham, Editor of the *Ross-shire Journal*; Willie Morrison, Editor of the *North Star* ; D. C. Thomson *The People's Journal*; Ordnance Survey *(Notes on Survey of 1872)*

Staff of Aberdeen University Special Library, Glasgow Museums (Scotland Street School), Inverness and Dingwall Public Libraries.

Janet Skrodzka for permission to use excerpts from her mother's book; the School Board, Parents' Association and Staff of Tore School; Kirsty Shaw, Andrina Gammie, Alasdair Cameron and Alison MacColl; Christina MacDonald who read the first draft and the other members of Ross-shire Writers for their encouragement.

Sketches: Julie MacIver for providing the sketches.

Photographs: The following companies for permission to use their work.

Andrew Allan, photographer, Alness; Ian Rhind, photographer, Culbokie; D.C. Thomson; The Press & Journal; Scholastic Souvenir Company; Fotek; Tempest Photography; National Union of Teachers; Eric Sutherland (for F.W. Urquhart).

Others who supplied photographs:

Steve Brown, Rena Cadger, Christobel Cameron, Jean Cameron, Val Clasper, Ann Dalgetty, Mr & Mrs R. Gillies, Betty Kirk, Iain Macdonald, Betty MacKay, Janet Munro, Ann Roots, John Ross , and Hamish Stevenson for his father's photographs (J.L. Stevenson).

The front cover photograph (top) was supplied by Margaret Olsen.

Every reasonable effort was made to track down ownership of other photographs used but I trust that where this has been unsuccessful the owner will be forgiving.

It has been difficult, even with much assistance, to put names to all the pupils in group photographs. I apologise if your name has been omitted or is incorrect.